More Praise for My Way Out

As a program, Jewell's *My Way Out* shows merit and is worthy of the same scrutiny Jewell gave to the procedures that shaped her program...

...Jewell states up front that she is not a medical professional, but a laywoman like '90s fitness guru Susan Powter who found a system that worked for her once she was able to understand her individuality as it related to fighting alcoholism. Like Powter, she shares her information for those searching for a cure adaptable to their own dispositions, people who have not found their salvation through 12-step programs. Jewell's honesty and forthright approach just might help a reader find his or her way out of addiction.

Foreword Reviews
www.forewordreviews.com

"Nutrition plays a critical role in recovery and Jewell's program incorporates all the key elements in a plan that is solid, straightforward and easy to follow. This multi-faceted system is sure to help many people. "

L. Kathleen Mahan, RD, CDE
Nutritional Counselor, Nutrition by Design and Co-Author,
Krause's Food, Nutrition and Diet Therapy, 11th ed., 2004
Seattle, WA

"The holistic approach combines powerful, customized self-hypnosis with other important therapeutic interventions. It's not surprising to me that the program works so well for those who suffer with alcohol addiction."

James H. Schmelter
Certified Hypnotherapist
San Francisco, CA

My Way Out

One Woman's Remarkable Journey in
Overcoming Her Drinking Problem and How
Her Innovative Program Can Help You
or Someone You Love

Roberta Jewell

Foreword by Linda Garcia, MD
Edited by Pete Spivey

capalopress
www.capalo.com

capalopress

Published by Capalo Press
www.capalo.com
3705 Arctic PMB 2571
Anchorage, Alaska 99503

The circumstances described in this book occurred as stated, however all names, except for that of Dr. Linda Garcia, MD, have been changed to protect the privacy of those who participated in the program or were affiliated with patients in the telling of the story.

Book cover design by Feed My Eyes, www.feedmyeyes.com
Printed by Gohram Printing, Rochester Washington, USA

Visit us online at www.mywayout.org

Library of Congress Cataloging-in-Publication Data
Jewell, Roberta.
  My way out : one woman's remarkable journey in overcoming her
    drinking problem and how her program can help you or someone you
    love / Roberta Jewell ; foreword by Linda Garcia ; edited by Pete Spivey.
    p. cm.
  Includes bibliographical references.
  ISBN 0-9762479-0-9 (alk. paper)
  1. Jewell, Roberta. 2. Alcoholics--Biography. 3. Alcoholics--Rehabilita-
    tion. 4. Hypnotism--Therapeutic use. I. Title.

RC565.J48 2005
362.292'092--dc22   2004024323

To my parents, who provided me the most wonderful life and an upbringing that gave me the skills I needed to overcome this problem. To my endlessly supportive husband, who cooked, cleaned and practically spoon fed me dinner over the keyboard as I raced toward publishing deadlines. To my remarkable, amazing, talented, brilliant, phenomenal—and very patient—kids, who mean more to me than anything in the world. And to Brenda, without whom none of this would have happened.

This book reflects the personal experience of the author. It is not intended as a substitute for professional assistance, but describes a program to be undertaken only under the supervision of a medical doctor or other qualified health care professional. The author and publisher disclaim any responsibility for adverse affects resulting directly or indirectly from information contained in this book.

The program described in My Way Out was developed and undertaken independently by the author and was done without the knowledge, consent, endorsement or approval of the manufacturers of any of the pharmaceutical, nutritional, or herbal products mentioned, or that of the researchers associated with the clinical trials involving medications referred to in the text. Specifically, topiramate is approved only for the treatment of people with seizures or migraine headaches and there are few systematic studies establishing its safety or efficacy in its use for patients with other disorders.

Contents

Preface

When a close friend of mine finally got the nerve, she asked me why I didn't publish this book under my real name. She speculated that given the success of the program I'd put together after exhaustive research and the interest it seemed to be generating, the book would do pretty well. Wouldn't I want to take some public ownership in that? And shouldn't I be willing to let go of the stigma associated with my past drinking?

I brushed it off at the time, but thinking about it later, realized the well-intentioned questions probably had more to do with shame than they did about fame. And that she didn't really understand I no longer felt stigmatized by my past behavior.

While I'm not proud of that fact that I drank to excess for much of my adult life, I am also utterly aware that the origins of my addiction were based primarily in a roll of the genetic dice. I wouldn't feel shameful about a predisposition to developing arthritis, cataracts or breast cancer. Nor would I hang my head over the fact that I was issued a receptor gene on a region of chromosome 15 that involves the activity of a brain chemical called GABRG3, which happened to increase my likelihood for an addiction to alcohol.

As I say in the book, I am not a physician, but I've

been knocking around the medical community for quite a while. Much of that time was spent researching and participating in another innovative, but completely unrelated, therapy for someone in my family. It was an exciting time, particularly to see the benefit that resulted from the brilliant work of research teams and clinicians who were passionate about helping their patients.

It also opened my eyes, however, to the incredibly demanding role of a blindly enthusiastic early adopter to a cutting edge therapeutic regimen. Although it was extremely effective, I was skewered by some who felt I was reckless in considering a therapy that hadn't stood the test of time. And in my eagerness to share our good fortune, my family was inundated with phone calls, emails, and television interviews. We were sought out by individuals from around the country seeking medical advice and support, particularly when they could not find local physicians to help them.

It seemed as if I blinked and eight years had passed. I was exhausted. (But by then, thankfully, our loved one's medical situation had completely turned around.)

I don't know if a person—an ordinary person anyway—should engage in that sort of effort more than once in a lifetime. Particularly when they have kids who are still at home, as I do, and want to preserve some sense of normalcy in their family life.

I also will not be surprised if this book will be looked upon as blasphemous by many in the traditional alcohol recovery movement. It allows those who are willing to do an honest assessment to select and pursue moderation as a reasonable drinking goal. It's not a new concept. But it approaches it in an entirely new way.

I am not afraid of this criticism, because I *know* this program works. I've experienced its benefits myself, and I've watched others who have been transformed by it. And thankfully, I've had the good fortune of working with Dr. Linda Garcia, a gifted and dedicated physician who is making the program available to her own patients and is sharing it with other health care providers so they may do the same.

If you follow the plan outlined in this book, I believe you will enjoy the same success of others who have gone before you. It can change your life. I firmly believe this program, or something very much like it, will eventually become a standard medical therapy to treat problem drinking. But if you don't want to wait until then, read the book, get to work, and prepare yourself for the most remarkable experience you've had since admitting to yourself that you have a problem with alcohol. You have worried and fretted and felt alone and sometimes desperate. I can only tell you I worked hard on this program that proved to be my way out, and I tell you with complete confidence it can be your way out, too. It is not frivolous; it is not quackery; it requires dedication on your part; and it simply will work for you if you are ready to change your life.

I'll be quietly watching from my anonymous vantage point as I enjoy private moments with my family, at times with a glass of wine, but never again worrying that this brain of mine will sabotage my efforts to avoid spiraling out of control.

It's a wonderful place to be. To drink with moderation, or quit drinking completely, if you wish. I invite you to join me here.

Foreword

By Linda Garcia, MD

My mother consumed alcohol most of her life. She had terrible asthma and would recount to me stories about how, on the days she had the most difficulty breathing, the family physician would instruct her to make a lemon toddy. This was a special concoction made up of lemon juice and strong tea, and she would lace it with a small amount of brandy. This was before the days of Albuterol or even Primatene® Mist, and therapeutically, it made sense. The strong tea was certainly a bronchodilator; the lemon and the sugar was a good demulcent; and the brandy was a sedative.

So, mom had this history of believing alcohol was good medicine because it was introduced to her at an early age. And it indeed gave some relief to her.

She was a good mother and always very supportive of me. She'd had a number of miscarriages in her attempts to have a child, so I knew I was wanted and clearly I was loved. But she drank, and as she got older, particularly by the time she reached menopause, she began to lose control over her drinking.

She had a difficult relationship with my father, who oversaw a rather oppressive household, even though he was not present most of the time. She stayed home; she did not drive, and she fulfilled her role as a stereotypical wife and mother of the 1950s. Dad felt he needed to work two jobs to support his family in a proper manner, and he spent more than three hours a day simply commuting between our suburban home and his Chicago offices.

Although my mother tried very hard to stop drinking, she could not, and the situation became increasingly intolerable. Many of my childhood memories include my father coming home late at night to find my mother passed out drunk.

The doctor tried to intervene after my father brought her in to treat her leg ulcers, which had begun to appear repeatedly. Now, of course, I understand they were classic symptoms and manifestations of vitamin deficiency and tissue fragility common with early alcoholic cirrhosis. But at the time we didn't know why she would get these recurring non-healing sores. Our family physician was very kind and competent and he told my father that drinking too much wine caused the sores. The doctor convened a family conference and urged us to admit her to the hospital where she could enter a sobriety program. My father and I implored her to do so; to get some help, have a sober life, and choose not to drink.

But she chose not to go. She announced that as far as she was concerned, alcohol was more important to her than either my dad or me. I thought that was horrible. To this day, it is a very painful memory, even though I understand the statement was made by someone in the clutches of a serious addiction. But we asked the doctor "Isn't there *something* you can do?" Doctors are supposed to have the answers, after all. He said he simply didn't have anything else to offer her; that he could not force her to enter a sobriety program against her will.

Her disease continued to progress after I went off to college. I'd already been interested and involved in health care, starting as a Candy Striper—an unlicensed nurse helper and volunteer—at Great Lakes Naval Station. It was the early 1960s and I remember seeing men who'd been injured in the conflicts leading up our full blown involvement in the Viet Nam war. I remember feeling somewhat functionless as a 16-year-old Candy Striper and always wanted to do more—to make a contribution. I admired individuals who worked in medicine and I wanted to help others as they did.

So I became a nursing assistant, went on to nursing school, and earned my license. I was a registered nurse for 18 years, seven of which I spent as a fire department emergency paramedic once I obtained additional training. I also spent time as an intensive care and flight nurse at a university hospital.

I decided to pursue a medical degree, and afterwards underwent an additional three years of training and specialization to become an internist. This is an area that emphasizes the diagnosis, management, and treatment of chronic medical issues. As internists, our job is to help patients achieve a better lifestyle through therapeutic intervention. The diseases we often treat include diabetes, hypertension, coronary artery diseases, and addictions, such as drug and alcohol abuse.

I was acutely aware of the consequences of substance abuse from both my family situation and my many years as a nurse and paramedic. Both made significant impressions on me. I have vivid recollections of what our EMT crews found waiting for us on those New Mexico highways as we raced in the dark, siren screaming, toward the State Trooper's bright glowing strobes.

We would discover drivers and passengers in distress, some dead, some alive and simply stunned, some terribly maimed and moaning in agony. Bodies were trapped in vehicles or thrown into the sagebrush and ditches. The crashed vehicles often were littered with opened containers of alcohol, strewn among the living and deceased. Those who'd been killed had already begun to turn cold and blue. The combined odor of blood, alcohol and motor oil, mixed with the stench of regurgitated stomach contents, purged upon impact, was pervasive. It was a sensory assault on a girl from the suburbs, and I will never, never forget it.

My experiences as a paramedic in which alcohol was a causative factor extended far beyond the highway horrors. Many homicides involved people who had been drinking, as well. So did the majority of suicides.

It wasn't until after I finished my medical education and I was a practicing physician that I realized just how much, given my earlier experiences, I wanted to find ways to help individuals overcome this disease of alcoholism. I had seen such graphic examples of the ravages it caused. I wanted to find a way to help patients achieve an improved lifestyle and have empowerment over their chronic health issues. I wanted to give them choices.

There's a tremendous emotional stigma that accompanies an addictive behavior. Most individuals who are diabetic or who have hypertension don't seem to be burdened with the same sort of shame or rejection issues. But those who suffer from alcohol and drug abuse are often viewed as lacking self-control. The same is true for the clinically obese, another group who suffers a chronic disease, but is often unfairly characterized as undisciplined or gluttonous.

And when an alcoholic goes out and binges, they're considered to be evil, out of control or simply unworthy of our care, even though medical therapeutic interventions have been slow to help them with their problem. That is not necessarily true for, say, a patient with congestive heart failure. That person is not considered to be evil or a failure because he binged on a bag of potato chips and suffered a heart failure episode due to an overload of salt.

Times are finally changing. Medication is now available for those who live with alcohol addiction. As outlined in this book, they can be administered in a less emotional manner and in conjunction with supplemental therapies to create a highly effective program. Many people will benefit from this approach.

I've prescribed the older generation medications, such as Antabuse®, which produces an aversion to alcohol if it is consumed. However, many patients simply don't want to take it because they know they will become sick if they drink. Another group of patients has learned how to modify administration of Antabuse® so the effects are not so harsh, and for this reason, it is not very effective. Naltrexone is another drug used for this purpose, but it can become ineffective relatively quickly.

The approach described in this book employs a new type of medication to help individuals gain control over a drinking problem without having to become completely abstinent. Many people do not want to say good-bye to alcohol. But they desperately want to learn how to control it and to become safe, social drinkers. Alcohol use is pervasive in our culture, and many people take great pleasure in moderate drinking.

Other individuals chose to be abstinent, and this program can also help them achieve that goal, as well.

Most of the patients I've followed simply want to have control. They want to enjoy a glass of wine with dinner, but they don't want to get sucked into that mode where they can't stop at one glass. They don't want to find themselves in a position where after the first drink their entire evening is spent in a tailspin of consuming more and more alcohol because a certain part of their brain just won't let them stop.

Utilizing the integrative therapies outlined in this

program, and under the care and counseling of a physician, one can now choose between gaining control over alcohol or abstaining completely. So it's really a two-in-one program: control or abstinence, whichever is most appropriate and desirable.

It also seems to fit within most individual's lifestyles much better than other therapies. In the past, I encouraged many patients to attend fellowship-based programs, whether they be religious counseling, Alcoholics Anonymous or other local support groups, most of which are modeled after AA.

But there are a significant number of people who do not wish to reveal in an open discussion setting they have an alcohol or drug problem. Or they feel they don't have the time in their busy schedules to attend group meetings on a regular basis. There are many reasons they are not comfortable in that therapeutic milieu, yet they wish to seek an opportunity to treat their problem and to gain control over their health issue. I've found that providing a secure, private environment, as this program does, has been very appealing to the patients I've offered it to.

We finally have an opportunity to provide effective tools to patients who suffer chronic addiction. As physicians, we can develop individualized therapeutic programs for them based on the important work conducted by researchers at the University of Texas START Center and later published in *The Lancet*, a highly respected journal of medical research. The START Center researchers demonstrated that a medication called topiramate can significantly curb cravings for alcohol. Combined with the other critical offerings in this book: hypnosis; herbal, nutritional and homeopathic supplements; exercise; and proper diet, we finally have a new avenue to treat patients who live with this disease.

Looking back at my mother's situation, I realize just how important gaining access to these tools has become to me and to my patients. Our family's doctor was a wonderful and compassionate physician. When he met with us and urged us to get her to the hospital for treatment, he took a great deal of time with a middle class family obviously in distress. He attempted to find a solution to a very bad situation. But he had neither the tools nor the solution. He had only himself, his best intentions to help us, and his input regarding a program available at the time that involved withdrawal and abstinence. And she rejected it.

After I left for college, I missed many of my mother's subsequent episodes, but of course when I would return home, I would note the disease had progressed. By then, my father was completely helpless to control her. As her drinking increased, she became more secretive and clever about procuring alcohol. She would take a taxi to the market to buy her elixir, or have a cabby deliver it to her door. This would infuriate my father who, in an effort to control her drinking, had forbidden her to leave the house.

When he retired, my dad was able to more carefully

supervise my mother's activities, although he was never completely capable of blocking alcohol from the home. He revealed to me that when they would go shopping—which they did twice a week—she would sometimes go to the alcohol section in the supermarket, grab a bottle, open it quickly, and take a swig. They were then required to purchase it. He was beside himself in his inability to control this type of behavior. But he also was mortified by the potential embarrassment at their local suburban supermarket, so ironically, he eventually began to buy the alcohol for her.

He could not comprehend any of this. He didn't drink himself. He disliked the taste and smell of liquor and couldn't understand why my mother could not stop herself from drinking it. And of course, he hated the disruption, embarrassment, and disorder it created in his family.

The situation with my mother and her disease got progressively worse, and although she had developed increased symptoms of cirrhosis, it was ultimately an alcoholic seizure coupled with a stroke that stopped her from drinking. She spent about six weeks in the hospital, but when she returned home, she resumed drinking. A few months later, she fell and broke her hip, which put her into a nursing home for approximately one year.

She finally returned home, but because of the stroke, paralysis on one side of her body, and fractured hip, she was no longer able to access alcohol. And my father would not provide it for her anymore. One of my most significant memories is of talking with her around that time—and by then she could no longer recognize who I was, and instead would refer to me as "that girl"—and would repeatedly ask me for just a little drink.

So my mother's memory of me as her daughter had passed with a series of seizures and a hypertensive stroke. She was unable to remember who I was, but was very much able to remember that she wanted that little drink.

My mother's health continued to decline, and she eventually succumbed to pneumonia at the age of 81. My father passed away exactly six months later, at the age of 85. They lived long, but their longevity was always overshadowed by alcoholism, and the contentment they could have had in those long years together was vastly compromised by my mother's drinking.

The same suffering still exists. A person becomes addicted to alcohol and it's followed by family disruption, myriad health problems, lost work productivity and many other issues. Overwhelming data from the National Institute of Health and other reputable organizations documents the pain and the price to problem drinkers, alcoholics, and their families.

But now we have an opportunity to reach out to those individuals and to offer them tools to achieve a desired level of drinking, or abstinence, and to help them be successful in the process.

My mother didn't have access to those tools, but my patients do. And with this book, so do you.

CHAPTER **ONE**

*There is no chance, destiny, no fate that
can circumvent or hinder or control the
firm resolve of a determined soul.*

–Ella Wheeler Wilcox

INTRODUCTION

*L*et me state up front: I am not a medical doctor. I
am not a PhD. I am not a researcher—officially, anyway.
In fact, my name is not even Roberta Jewell, but you don't
really need to know my name because you're already familiar with my circumstances: you or someone you love
has struggled with the debilitating, painful reality of life as
a problem drinker.

Where did the problem come from? Well, what are
the roots of any addictive behavior? I assume it was primarily genetic in my case: I was adopted as a toddler and
understand that both of my biological parents had "drug
and alcohol issues" but I don't know the details.

My adoptive parents provided a warm and loving
home for my brother, sister and me, and were what I would
consider to be social drinkers, the kind I would yearn to
become later in life. They used alcohol in moderation. Dad
would often pop open a beer after a long day at the job—

typically before starting an after-work second shift building our new house, developing the property in which they'd invested, or simply putting in all the hard hours it took to grow the family business. Mom usually had a cocktail only when we went out for a special occasion.

It didn't seem like a problem for me in high school or college—it was called partying back then and everyone did it. My grades were good and I saved my fun for the weekends, just like other kids. Looking back, I think I enjoyed drinking more than many of my peers, but I was generally enthusiastic about most things and it certainly didn't seem like cause for concern.

I married a man who liked to drink as much as I did. By the time I was in my mid-to late twenties it had pretty much become a daily affair for us, and frankly, I was more comfortable with someone who didn't make me feel guilty about it. We were together six years before we started a family, and we enjoyed those years fishing, camping, running a new business, and spending time with friends. Drinking not only didn't interfere with our life, it seemed to enhance it.

By the time the first of our babies came along, it had become clear to me that abstinence was not going to be easy, but I gave it my best shot. I held out for the entire term of the first pregnancy, but despite what I knew about alcohol passing into breast milk, I started drinking an occasional cocktail at night while nursing my first child.

When I became pregnant a second time, I again forced myself off the booze—at least for the first three months, which I knew were most critical. I allowed myself an infrequent glass of wine or light cocktail towards the end of my pregnancy when the cravings got the better of me.

When that baby was born with a serious genetic disorder, I was absolutely devastated, and convinced it was all my doing—that one of those drinks had somehow caught up with me—even though a world renowned expert in the disease assured me that wasn't the case.

Our third child was not planned and arrived unbelievably soon after the second (healthy as a horse, thankfully). But it didn't take long before I found it was all I could do to keep the bottle at bay. I was bending under the pressure of raising three young children, dealing with the burdensome debt of a failing business, nurturing a youngster with a disability, and managing what would prove to be early symptoms of clinical depression.

I retreated further into the numbing effects of alcohol, which seemed to relieve the agonizing pain and stress of my everyday life, if only temporarily.

But I hid it well. As everyone around me marveled at my strength and fortitude, I found solace at night in the sweet drinks I sipped from my endless supply of eight-dollar bottles of vodka.

Over the next decade or so my family situation improved significantly. I worked ceaselessly to better our child's medical condition, and it paid off thanks to the tireless research of dedicated clinicians who developed new therapeutic protocols to treat the disease. Much of it was largely unknown to the medical community as a whole and I became involved in disseminating information about these new treatments.

I also embarked upon a new career path, eventually earning an executive management position, and then other rewarding opportunities came my way. Our family finances slowly crept into a healthier state, and my husband, who agreed to work part-time and manage the household—having always been a superior and more agreeable house-keeper, cook and children's chauffeur than I—provided solid and endless logistical support to the kids and me. Despite our ups and downs, he was, and remains, my rock and a source of endless strength and humor.

One thing that did not change, however, was my drinking. It actually grew worse. My tolerance for liquor had increased and I seemed to need more drinks, or at least stronger ones.

Some mornings my head ached from the previous evening's round of drinking. At times, I even drove my car when under the influence, and occasionally either missed a day of work, or watched my productivity suffer because I couldn't concentrate. I found myself making promises to the kids that alcohol prevented me from keeping, or fighting with my husband and sometimes becoming irrational.

Although I was still pretty good at hiding my problem from those around me, I feared it was only a matter of time before I would do something very stupid after too many drinks.

I was, to put it as plainly as I can, becoming somebody I despised.

I had tried to stop, or at least slow down, so many times. Over the years, it seemed as if I had read every book on the subject and investigated every possible conventional and non-traditional recovery therapy I could get my hands on.

Anyone who knows me well would tell you that I'm a proficient researcher—particularly when it comes to medical matters, a skill I developed when I was desperately trying to find help beyond the conventional and ineffective treatment that traditional medicine offered our second child. Dozens of family members and friends since have called upon me to help them investigate a wide range of afflictions and diseases, and I'm very proud of what I've helped uncover for them and the positive impact it has had on the lives of the people I care about.

But nothing I had found was helping me solve *my own* serious health problem, which continued to deteriorate.

Then an incredible turn of events changed my life. After nearly 20 years of aggressively conducting all that research, I was graced by what I can only describe as some sort of supreme serendipity, and the solution to my problem dropped perfectly and profoundly into my lap.

After all the unproductive attempts to rid myself of my misery, I stumbled upon early results of innovative clinical research with an oral medication called topiramate for treating alcoholism. I found an article buried in a newspaper in the spring of 2003 that reported a study by physicians at the University of Texas Health Science Center at

San Antonio. Their report concluded that half of the alcoholics in their study who were given the medicine either quit drinking completely or cut back sharply. Within months, more news stories and Internet postings hailed it as a major scientific breakthrough.

Many of the popular press articles on this report focused on the medication's unexpected weight loss properties. I suppose our current fixation on fad diets and the relentless stories about America's problem with obesity makes that understandable. All I know is I didn't care about any of that; my curiosity was strongly piqued about the drug's apparent proven ability to curb drinking. And I dug in on the research.

By the time the animated morning news anchors were introducing stories about the drug on their network programs in the fall, I already knew more about the subject than most of the physicians in my community.

I had launched my own personal research campaign and discovered that topiramate was manufactured by Ortho-McNeil Pharmaceuticals and marketed as Topamax® by its parent company, Johnson and Johnson. Sold primarily as a medication to treat epilepsy, Topamax® also is prescribed off-label to treat nicotine addiction, bi-polar disorder, binge eating, and other ailments. (Off-label prescribing allows physicians to provide medications to patients suffering from conditions other than those the medicine was specifically tested for in clinical trials. It is a common and acceptable practice.)

I discovered the drug had an impressive track record, and was reported to have minimal side effects. Its success in treating problem drinkers in Texas, however, clearly was based on the patients' willingness and ability to augment the drug regimen by attending an onsite treatment facility. And to participate in a carefully controlled program in which medical professionals could conduct and analyze lab work, provide medical screening, issue medication, and offer behavioral therapy sessions. All those supporting components were concluded to be the key to the drug's success.

The Internet message boards I'd found with postings by those who were prescribed the medication for off-label use also provided valuable information to me, including real-world descriptions of temporary side effects I might experience. After weighing both the clinical and anecdotal (and confident the relatively benign and temporary side effects could be addressed with the appropriate nutritional supplements), I ordered a month's supply from an online pharmacy whose requirements for prescriptions were somewhat lenient. I didn't care to get my doctor involved yet—who knew if she'd approve? I was an adult, after all, and I'd done my research.

Also, I had adequate experience in buying pharmaceuticals on the web and keeping my private matters private, so it didn't take long to find a company who stocked the medication and was willing to oblige. I eagerly anticipated the arrival of my package from its offshore source as I prepared for a business conference and visit with "Brenda", a good friend and former college roommate in a neighboring state.

It was at a small dinner party at Brenda's that the subject of addiction fortuitously arose (not mine of course—who would ever have guessed?).

I'd been thinking earlier about the topiramate research I'd done as I forced myself to s-l-o-w-l-y sip the weak whiskey soda her husband had graciously offered me. Why did it take everyone else so long to finish *their* drinks, anyway? I was grateful for the cocktail, but much preferred to make them myself when traveling—I never left home without a bottle in my bag.

Now at the dinner table and midway into our meal, just as I was calculating the status of that second bottle of Merlot sitting on the kitchen counter, Brenda shared a story about her sister-in-law, who'd had an interesting experience several years earlier after attending a hypnosis seminar.

The sister-in-law apparently suffered a ferocious smoking habit most of her adult life, had been unsuccessful in every attempt to quit, and wondered if hypnosis might help. She went to a hypnosis presentation, but found she didn't care for its carnival slickness, or the hypnotist himself, for that matter, and concluded it was all "a bunch of hooey."

In fact, she was so incensed at the $55 she had paid, she walked out and vented her anger to my friend over the cell phone on her drive home. Brenda calmed her down and insisted she listen to the tape that came with the price of admission. Against her better judgment, her sister-in-law did just that, playing the tape after she relaxed and was ready for bed. She woke up the next morning to find her cigarette craving completely gone, and swears she has never fired one up again. Of course, no one was more surprised than the disgruntled customer herself.

Now, I love a good dinnertime story as much as the next person—but I felt confident this wasn't a tale, because I know Brenda too well, and she's simply incapable of lying.

But what really struck me at that moment was the fact that after so many years of research, I had completely overlooked hypnosis as a potentially powerful therapeutic treatment for addiction.

It also occurred to me that it could complement a seemingly unrelated medicinal therapy like topiramate, and together, perhaps they could perform a critically important dance upon the neurons of a brain—of my brain, for God's sake—in modifying behavior.

Combined with the other essential weapons I was amassing in my research arsenal—an assortment of vitamins, minerals, amino acids and herbs I had earlier identified as effective in treating alcohol cravings—and a simple exercise regimen I would employ for its obvious physical and emotional rewards, I became convinced I just may have found the means to defeat the demons I had been battling most of my adult life.

I had already fine-tuned and printed out the formula of nutritional supplements, topiramate dosing and an exercise schedule before leaving for my conference. But until that moment at the dinner with Brenda, it had never occurred to me to consider incorporating hypnotherapy as a behavior modification component. When the idea dawned, it seemed a perfect addition to round out the program, and might even emulate some of the benefits patients in the original clinical trial had enjoyed, as it could provide a foundation for supporting the fundamental behavioral changes that were about to occur.

Of paramount importance to me was the knowledge I was on to something that offered the ability to fight—and win—this battle in the privacy of my own home. Treatment in a public or clinical setting was simply not an option I cared to pursue.

How incredible, it seemed, that after searching for a solution for so many years that the two final puzzle pieces—topiramate and hypnotherapy—would come together so seamlessly and within a matter of weeks. It felt like nothing less than some sort of divine intervention.

Somehow I knew before I even began this home-grown therapeutic program that it would work—but I had no idea just how effectively, and how quickly.

At the time, I had done enough research about the neurological underpinnings of the human brain to understand that pharmacological agents could help and, in fact, had already been developed by the mid 1990s to help mitigate the craving for alcohol.

One of the most promising medications, naltrexone, had begun to offer hope for those with drinking problems and was being used at recovery centers throughout the United States. In fact, I had even managed to persuade a sympathetic young psychiatrist to provide me with a prescription years earlier and was thrilled to learn that it did, in fact, reduce the craving. For a while, anyway. And though I'd promised to do so, I ignored his advice about seeking counseling while taking it, as I'd found it difficult enough simply getting myself into his office in the first place.

Alcoholics Anonymous may have seemed the obvious route, but it was out of the question for me, as reputable a program I understood it to be. I didn't want to quit drinking entirely—I just wanted to gain control over it. And unfortunately, I hadn't had any luck with programs like Moderation Management, an approach that required 30 days of abstinence, which I had been incapable of achieving.

So naltrexone, the wonder drug prescribed years earlier overseas and for which I'd eagerly awaited FDA approval, was finally available, but just as the psychiatrist had predicted, it was no magic bullet. Unaccompanied by supportive therapies, its much touted powers soon lost their luster, and I quickly learned that it would take much more than a little white pill at lunchtime to reverse a lifetime of drinking.

It was a painful lesson, and while I was disheartened as I found myself back to my old habits, in hindsight I realize it was a critical lesson. It reinforced my basic belief that this problem of mine—and millions like me—was very much biochemical in nature, and that perhaps pharmacology could, in the proper setting, offer a powerful means to help flip off that damn dopamine switch, the trigger to the chemical wreaking havoc in my brain.

But back to Brenda's dinner party. One guest, intrigued by the hypnosis discussion, mentioned she had once seen a news program about the success of therapeutic hypnosis. I remarked that it seemed as if all kinds of new therapies were being developed to treat addictions.

I said I had recently read an article about an epilepsy drug. "I think it's called Topamax®," I offered, "and it's supposed to help people with drinking problems." But nobody bit, so I dropped it. We eventually wrapped up the evening and the rest of the group headed home. I was staying the night and hoped to finesse another drink under the time-honored custom of a nightcap.

Thankfully, Brenda invited me to join her for a late-night, girls-only cocktail. Her cat weaved between us and we began to catch up on our lives once we settled on her couch with our drinks.

"So what do you know about this Topamax®?" she asked me, steely-eyed, out of the blue, an hour later into a completely unrelated conversation.

It hit me like a truck.

I was flabbergasted to learn as we talked late into the night, that like me, she struggled with a similar secret drinking problem. Who would ever have guessed that this successful, beautiful, highly respected mother, wife, and working woman suffered the same private pain as me? Distance had separated us since our intimate days as college roommates but we had remained close friends, and I thought I knew all sides of her.

For the first time in our lives, we shared our stories, and we shared them with someone who understood, because we were both living the lie. What a relief to know that we were not alone. I had never told anyone how miserable I was because of my drinking—even my husband of 19 years, who despite knowing how desperate I was to change my life, really had no idea how truly unhappy I had become because of my addiction to alcohol.

We stayed up the entire night and I told Brenda about the endless searching I'd done over the years in hopes of curing myself; about the numerous therapies and medications and nutritional supplements I'd tried; about my reluctance to join AA or to enter a program within a clinical setting. I told her about all books I'd read and the research I'd conducted and that despite the fact this was the single most important goal in my life—because surely I would not live to see my children grow up if I continued to drink at my current pace—that nothing I'd tried had worked.

So, now, along with the medication, nutritional supplements and exercise regimen, I wanted to research and consider enhancing the plan with therapeutic hypnosis. I proposed that each therapy had a powerful and important contribution to make. Topiramate was clearly effective in curbing craving—the research had indicated participants in the Texas study were six times more likely than those taking a placebo to abstain from alcohol.

In addition, I would augment the medication with the herbs and supplements I had learned about (and tried myself) over so many years. For instance, I would include glutamic acid, which converts to L-glutamine, and has been shown effective in reducing the desire to drink; I'd use the herb milk thistle, which is said to repair some of the damaging effects of alcohol on the liver; and I'd incorporate kudzu extract, which is believed to significantly decrease the craving for alcohol.

Some of the supplements, I would later learn, would even offset the bothersome side effects of the topiramate. As for exercise, it would also play an important role in both overcoming symptoms of depression and in releasing endorphins, both of which have been proven to help reduce the incidence of relapse in patients recovering from addiction.

So how would hypnosis fit into the mix and would it enhance the success of this program?

I soon learned the answer. I can state with complete and utter honesty that the irrepressible desire to drink to excess, that gentle nagging that emerged in young adulthood and mushroomed over 20 years into an ugly and uncontrollable craving, quickly and completely disappeared.

The transformation took place quietly and painlessly and was extinguished, quite frankly, within a matter of days. I was dumbfounded, because as much I wanted to believe that it would work—having experimented with minor versions and various elements of this program over the past dozen or so years and expecting at least some favorable results from the cocktail of amino acids and herbs that often promote detoxification and craving reduction— I was nevertheless astounded by such immediate results.

I knew from the very first day I started the program that my life was about to be transformed.

Brenda, who was as enthusiastic as I was to try this out, was preparing for a family vacation, so was unable to begin until a few weeks later. She had a hard time believing my results were so dramatic. And as wonderfully supportive as she was over those early long distance phone calls from her trip (I knew she was struggling to believe me—but I don't think *I* would have believed me, either) it wasn't until she returned home and started the program herself that she learned of its power and how swiftly it would kick in.

Her desire to drink plummeted within days, and she was ecstatic at finding, as I did, she had finally gained control over her problem. She remains today free of the craving that once controlled her life.

We vowed each year we would celebrate our mutual "birthday"—the birth of the new us—that took place on a special night when we revealed to one another our most solemn secret and resolved to fix it.

I found the immediacy of the results startling, to say the least. My craving for alcohol was gone from the first day. And I mean simply, totally gone. I could practically hear the prison gates being lifted. The utter ease with which I was able to abstain from drinking in the first week completely surprised me.

I knew enough about the "placebo effect" to wonder if that was at play—if I were only *imagining* that it was working so well. Nothing like that had ever happened with anything else I'd tried; only the naltrexone had nipped the craving in the bud so quickly, but again, that was short-lived.

Clinical studies indicated the peak effects of Topamax® are typically achieved at the sixth and eighth week, so that couldn't explain it either. I had to believe the combination of adjunct therapies, including the supplements and customized hypnotherapy program, was resulting in much more effective results.

And as captivated as I was by what I'd heard about the smoker's hypnosis experience—as well as the body of scientific research I found supporting hypnotherapy as a therapeutic approach to treating addiction—this came as a shock to someone who had never been hypnotized. In fact, I was fairly confident I was an unlikely candidate. (I've since learned that addictive personalities are in fact often *more* likely to accept hypnotic suggestion).

The term "hypnotherapy" is a bit of a misnomer in its use here. I sought a self-hypnosis recording because I felt more comfortable doing behavior modification in my own home. I evaluated several commercially available audiotapes and CDs but was concerned most would not pack the punch I was looking for.

As I conducted my research, I learned how hypnotic intervention had been used over the centuries to alter behavior, but something else also occurred to me: it would behoove me to find a system that included other proven behavior modification therapies to augment a simple self-hypnosis program. As much as I wanted the hypnosis to work, I'd be foolish to disregard the data indicating it was simply ineffective for some people. What if I were one of them?

I wasn't going to take any chances. Clearly, some of the other techniques had respectable success rates, and if I were find one that *combined* them...why not put them together in the same program? I searched for, reviewed and evaluated products until I came upon one that incorporated hypnotherapy, visualization, autogenic therapy (a meditative technique) and positive affirmations, and also allowed a high level of customization, which I intuitively felt was key to a successful program.

Ultimately I ended up working with a highly experienced hypnotherapist who has a significant background in behavior modification and employs the techniques described, as well as other particularly effective hypnotic methods. I wrote a script to address my specific drinking issues and desired outcomes, and he weaved the content into his recorded hypnotherapy and subliminal sessions, which he sent to me on a set of CDs. Once I had the recordings in hand, I added my own "mini" positive suggestions, visualizations, and affirmations, which I prepared in advance and used on a regular basis.

It turned out to be the makings of some incredibly powerful behavioral modification therapy. There is no doubt in my mind that the combined multiple techniques dramatically improved the therapeutic value of the entire system.

I am also confident the comprehensive program of nutritional supplements, medication and hypnotherapy that I developed for myself and later shared with others will work for you or someone you care about, but only if it is carried out in much the same way and in partnership with a physician or other qualified health care professional.

Anyone knowledgeable about recovery will also attest to the obvious value of nutrition, exercise, and a healthy lifestyle. But one thing you will not find here is a lecture about strict adherence to a diet plan—you'll be making enough changes as it is. I would, however, *strongly* encourage you to cut back on sugar. This will help keep your blood sugar stable and play a strong role in reducing your craving for alcohol. I also recommend you significantly increase your intake of water, especially at the onset of the program.

That's it for diet lectures—at least for now—and the reason is this: you'll be going through a tremendous and positive transformation, one that is physical, emotional, psychological, even spiritual, I found. There's an awakening that is difficult to describe.

But there is one aspect of the transformation I *can* put into words: the self-loathing ends, the insidious feeling that sneaks up on you after so many years as punishment for the addiction you've been powerless to control. It's a big, big change to walk away from that mindset.

I believe it's okay to indulge in occasional treats while

you're making such a fundamental adjustment to your lifestyle, and if you follow the guidelines outlined in this book you'll be fine; just don't sabotage yourself in the process. If you are truly motivated, you'll know the difference between an indulgence and returning to behavior that leads to abandoning the program.

Here's the other good news: (I've saved the best for last, at least for those of you looking to drop some weight). Topiramate probably will reduce your appetite considerably and help you slim down, a reasonable goal for many of us whose waistlines reflect years of excessive drinking.

Those who take it for a variety of disorders tend to lose ten, 20, up to 35 or more pounds. I was delighted and surprised to lose 27 pounds in three months, and I have kept it off. But if you do not wish to lose weight, be sure to make accommodations in your diet in the other direction. This actually became problematic for Brenda, who unlike me, is quite petite, and found herself extremely challenged to keep her weight *up*. Truly a problem many women would love to have!

A number of people assumed I was aggressively dieting because my weight loss was so dramatic. Consequently, I received endless comments and questions by well-intentioned family members and friends. I came up with all kinds of excuses as to why I'd lost the weight—I went from size 13 to 8—and eventually decided to pick up a copy of the latest diet fad book so I had a pat answer.

Today, I consider myself a social drinker but fully understand this program may be hugely unpopular with many in the recovery movement who have legitimate concerns that excessive drinkers—particularly medium and late stage alcoholics—can never drink moderately. Some say "you cannot turn a pickle back into a cucumber."

Frankly, I believe there's some merit to that argument, and for that reason I must emphasize *this program is specifically geared for early and medium stage problem drinkers who are highly motivated to control their drinking or quit drinking completely*.

If you are, indeed, an advanced medium or late stage alcoholic, you will undoubtedly benefit from many aspects of this program, but will most likely need to seek more aggressive intervention in a clinical setting. If that's the case, please get help immediately, but read this book nonetheless, talk to your health care provider about it, and adapt what you can to your medical treatment plan.

I've included some guidelines in the appendix about the progressive drinking phases from early to late stage alcoholism. If you're unsure about where you fall in the spectrum your doctor can help, and as stated at the front of this book, *do not begin this program without the supervision and approval of your health care provider*. This therapy will be most successful if carried out under the guidance of a medical professional, and it's critical you are evaluated for any potential health risks before you begin.

Your physician will also be the one to provide you with a prescription for topiramate, which is used much more frequently to treat problem drinking—and a host of other ailments—than when I first ordered my meds online.

I now work closely with my doctor, who handles my medication, and has monitored all facets of the program for me.

I've given much consideration to the fact that my own personal goal was moderation, not abstinence. An honest self-assessment will reveal what is most appropriate for you. You must bear in mind that the longer you have been drinking and the more serious your drinking problem, the more unrealistic the goal of moderate drinking may be, even with this marvelously effective program on your side.

Clearly, abstinence, while it may seem less appealing to you, may very well be a safer option. Please keep that in mind because your goal, after all, is to save your life. For more information about the benefits and risks of moderate drinking, see what the National Institute on Alcohol Abuse and Alcoholism has to say in Appendix A of this book.

I obviously had a long history of drinking when I started the program and was at my all time drinking peak when I began. Nonetheless, I opted for moderation—with a backup plan of abstinence if I couldn't pull it off—since I love wine with meals, I enjoy social drinking, and given a choice between abstaining or drinking moderately, I find the latter makes life a lot more enjoyable. Now, periodically, I quit drinking for extended periods just to make sure I'm still in control.

Others will take another path because through no fault of their own, they will never be able to drink socially.

So for them, and perhaps for you, complete alcohol cessation is the only realistic goal.

And that's fine—wonderful, in fact—because this program can help you achieve an outcome of zero drinking in a way that nothing else probably will. In fact, the researchers who developed the topiramate program in Texas are emphatic that abstinence was the primary objective of their work, and they noted one of the benefits of the medication was the ability to safely dispense it while test subjects were still winding down on their drinking.

I am absolutely convinced the comprehensive therapies outlined in this program will release you from the craving more quickly and effectively than medication or group-based talking therapy alone.

And if Alcoholics Anonymous or another fellowship-based option is right for you, I'm confident this program will help ensure your success when used concurrently.

This book is merely an honest reflection of my personal experience—obviously not that of a clinical researcher or a professional who's devoted her career to the treatment and recovery of alcoholics. (It is one of the reasons it is imperative you work with your doctor when you begin this program.)

But it reminds me: Brenda and I discussed the term "alcoholic" in some detail, and quite frankly, weren't sure *what* to call ourselves. We knew we had a problem with alcohol, but we didn't consider ourselves in denial when we discarded the label "alcoholic." Many, I'm sure, would argue that point. I suspect my drinking was more serious than hers. I failed every one of those tests I had ever taken in the books and magazines asking, "Are You an Alcoholic?" or "Do You Have a Drinking Problem?"

Frankly, deciding what to call it wasn't that big of deal to me, although I never cared to stand up in an AA meeting and proclaim it to a room full of strangers.

Clinically, I certainly met the criteria of an alcoholic and in my heart I knew I had a problem that needed fixing. Yet for some reason, Brenda and I both took issue with a label that had been painted with such a broad brush, and sure enough, I later learned that some of the newer research supports what our instincts told us: we, along with an estimated 12 million others in this country, might more appropriately fit the profile of "problem drinkers."

We were gainfully employed, involved in steady, long-term relationships, and our drinking problem had not yet spun completely out of control. However, like those who suffered alongside us, we acknowledged it was indeed destroying our lives.

According to recent statistics, there are four problem drinkers for every "hard core" alcoholic in the United States, and because of the sheer numbers, this population is at the heart of many of our social and economic troubles, from drinking while driving, to lost work productivity, to family dysfunction.

Yet problem drinkers don't feel they fit the stereotype of a traditional alcoholic and are reluctant to seek conventional approaches to treatment. Why should they? We didn't. So why would you?

I am convinced that if you follow the program outlined in this book it will help you overcome your craving for alcohol and control your drinking or quit entirely, if that's your goal.

When I started it, I carefully followed the oral topiramate dosing according to the exact schedule outlined in the clinical trial developed by researchers at the University of Texas Health Science Center, but without their knowledge, consent, or endorsement, or that of Johnson and Johnson, Ortho-McNeil or anyone else—I want to be clear that I did this as a free-lancer.

At the time of this writing, this medication is not approved by the FDA for treatment of alcoholism, just as it is not approved by the FDA (but is often used) for treating, bipolar disorder, binge eating, or anything other than epilepsy or migraine headaches, and again, if prescribed by your physician, it will be done so for off-label use—again, a common medical practice.

The landmark study regarding topiramate's effectiveness in treating alcoholics was published in the May 17, 2003 issue of *The Lancet*, a well-respected medical journal. You can request a copy from your local library or purchase the article from Lancet's website. I've included news stories and other information about topiramate on the research link found at my website: www.mywayout.org, as well.

Please be advised that Ortho-McNeil Pharmaceuticals issued a drug warning in September 2001 stating that in rare cases some patients taking topiramate for migraines reported blurred vision or eye pain within the first month.

I say again, it is imperative that you see your physician before starting this program, and report to him or her immediately if you experience these symptoms, as they could lead to serious vision problems.

At the same time I started the topiramate dosing, I began listening to the hypnotic CDs and taking the nutritional supplements. I'd planned on commencing the exercise regimen—simply walking briskly outdoors or using a treadmill twenty to thirty minutes, three times a week— but I came down with what I thought was the flu, so gave myself a reprieve of a few days.

However, by the following week I was feeling so incredibly energized by the vitamins and detoxification ("What is *in* these vitamins?" Brenda asked me when she started) that I created two 30-minute power walking CD's from my music collection and found myself enthusiastically sweating to Tina Turner, Annie Lennox and Melissa Etheridge on a regular basis. I even had the hypnotist add a subliminal overlay on my exercise CDs for increased benefit.

I've since learned the exercise program can be reduced to a 15 or 20 minute activity, which some participants tell me better accommodates their busy schedules.

You'll see from some of the entries Brenda and I emailed each other and used as personal journals just how different life became for us over the course of only a few weeks. By the time I had finished and enjoyed success with the first phase of the program—medication, inten-

sive vitamin supplementation, and concurrent hypnotherapy sessions—I knew I was on to something. After six
months, and continued progress, my life had changed dramatically. A year later, it was clear to me I would never
again be ruled by the addiction I felt had nearly stolen my
soul and robbed me of my future.

I wanted others to know about this therapy so I quietly began sharing my success with those who needed help.
I assumed there were thousands in my town alone who
were fighting a similar battle or knew other problem drinkers who were motivated to change (and motivation is absolutely *crucial*). Certainly there had to be millions who,
like me, had found themselves consumed by a disease that
was ravaging their lives, but who were unwilling to seek
help through traditional means.

At this point, I had also "confessed" to a trusted friend
and highly regarded physician in our community about
what I was up to. He was intrigued, and then very supportive of my work once he learned the details, read the
data, and saw the results. In fact, he had been clinically
trained in therapeutic hypnosis and had used it successfully as an alternative to traditional anesthesia for some of
his pediatric patients.

He introduced me to another prominent physician
in our region and one who was very familiar with recovery issues. An internist with decades of experience, she
had too often seen first hand that traditional medical approaches were often ineffective in treating addiction. She
felt my system had merit and was enthusiastic about adopt-

ing a more integrative, holistic approach to recovery.

And *I* was enthusiastic about adopting a more clinical approach to the demand, as word was getting out. As thrilled as I was about the success stories, I had no desire to become known around town as the rehab queen. I had my own family, career and life to tend to.

A close friend had already warned me to tread carefully; that I may be taking on more than I could handle in sharing the program. I live in a relatively small community with an extended family, some members of whom are vigilantly private.

But it seemed almost criminal to keep it a secret. The program had worked so well and was incredibly easy to follow. For me it was it was downright enjoyable and I loved it so much, at one point I was concerned that I might be trading in one addiction for another! The hypnotherapy CDs in particular, provided a level of relaxation I had never experienced before. And the overall program completely transformed my life.

Clearly the problem I had overcome was one that millions of others suffered. I felt compelled to share it.

The program is effective and straightforward. Medication acts on pathways of the brain to curb the desire to drink. Hypnotherapy provides positive and powerful behavior modification. Nutritional supplements handle detoxification and cravings. A simple regimen of exercise increases fitness, emotional stamina, and helps prevent relapse.

The combined effect of the supplements, exercise and

self-hypnosis can all address potential, but usually temporary, side effects of the medication that affect some individuals.

It all works together in the most remarkable way.

To say I am ecstatic to be free of the inexhaustible cravings that once ruled my life would be an absolute understatement. All I ever really wanted to be was "normal." I wanted to think about alcohol, as Brenda, my dear friend who joined me on this journey said, like you would about butter, a humorous but very accurate analogy, really. I didn't race home to eat butter, I didn't think about it during the day and abuse it at night—and it certainly didn't make me feel remorseful in the morning. At times when dieting, I wouldn't allow it at my table. But it sure was nice to have a moderate amount of it in my life.

I now consider myself a run-of-the-mill, average social drinker. But there's nothing mundane about having that vicious craving out of my life!

I doubt if anyone who has never battled a drinking problem can truly understand how wonderfully liberating it is to say "no thank you"—and mean it—when the waiter visits your table to check on everyone's drinks. To see the same bottle of wine in the refrigerator or cabinet after several days. To find your glass left unfinished when cleaning up the next morning. To drive home from work without stopping at the liquor store, where you once prayed your neighbors wouldn't see you once again with your bottle at the register.

It's difficult to describe the sheer joy of such simple

pleasures.

And as a parent there can be no greater reward than to know that you have pulled yourself out of the grip of addiction. To me, that was absolutely the most difficult and perplexing thing to grasp. How could I possibly have allowed myself to drink to excess—to let the booze to get the better of me—when I loved my kids so deeply? But that's the power an addiction gradually gains over you. That's how much it controls your world.

Surely, one of the lowest points in my life came when my 14-year-old daughter confessed she had poured out the bottle of vodka in my liquor cabinet and filled it with water as she secretly tried to save me from myself. I thank God those days are over.

Obviously, all facets of this program have not been scientifically tested nor peer-reviewed, and the results described within these pages (outside of those cited as otherwise) are anecdotal. However, I do hope that one day this program will be rigorously reviewed, tested, and refined by experts—especially once a significant number of individuals have tried and experienced success with it.

I believe it's also critical we provide more options regarding treatment venues, because I am confident the majority of problem drinkers will select the privacy of their own homes over a public setting.

As I write this I take a sip of water from the wine goblet next to me and I'm reminded of the many popular and well intentioned books I've read over the years about how to stop, control, or moderate my drinking. I'm quite confident I started most of them with a cocktail in hand—convinced I would begin the next day anew, inspired by what I was about to learn in the wisdom of the pages before me.

How odd, it seems, that I—who never aspired to write a book, but merely hoped to find one to help me fix my misbehaving brain—would one day see my own work there next to those familiar texts, describing a successful program that completely turned my life around.

This is the story of how I found my way out.

May it also be yours.

CHAPTER **TWO**

*Do not lose courage in considering your
own imperfections but instantly set about
remedying them—every day begin the
task anew.*

—Saint Francis de Sales

THE JOURNEY

*W*e learn so much from one another's experiences, and
that's why Brenda and I felt it was important to document
this journey, even before we formally began. I've included
a number of excerpts from our e-mail correspondence,
many of which I later found extremely valuable, as it reminded me of some details I'm sure I would have otherwise forgotten. I've never kept a journal so it was an
interesting exercise, and I hope it's one you'll consider doing,
as well. I also hope you'll find something that touches you
in these casual and candid letters shared between friends
as we embarked down this most remarkable path together.

Roberta: Friday Night in the House of Booze

*Friday. I always welcome Friday because it's the beginning
of the weekend and means it's okay to drink. Wait, I drink every
night, just more on Fridays, I suppose. One Saturday morning a*

couple months ago I was so hung over I figured the only way I could make it go away was to have a drink, so I made a Bloody Mary, put it in a coffee cup, and drank it with breakfast. I wonder if the kids thought it was strange that I had ice cubes in there, but they didn't ask. I was reminded of a test I took to see if you have a drinking problem and one of the clues was drinking in the morning.

My God, why in the world do I always take those tests? Every time I see one I take it—like I don't KNOW! Like maybe this one is going to prove something different... "Yep, that's right...I do NOT have a drinking problem, thank goodness I finally found a legitimate test."

So it's Friday, and I know exactly how this evening will evolve, from the first sip, to the second drink, nice buzz going by the third, then another, and making plans or promises to the kids before I'm through. Saturday morning brings with it the dreaded remorse. I'm dehydrated in both body and soul and have an achy feeling in the back of my eyes. The previous evening will be a fuzzy memory, and I'll suffer that familiar guilt, issue an apology to the kids...sorry mom was so tired last night—been working all these late hours and all—what was it again I said we were going to do today?

Brenda: Priming the Pump

Just had a great long bath. How fun it is to take a soaker in my big tub with a trashy Star magazine. Love to see who has the nicest skin at 40, hee hee. Before running up the flight of stairs, I glance at the clock. It showed 5 p.m....not quite wine time (with Peter home, it isn't). So, I grabbed a Corona and headed upstairs. I have always loved the "primer" drink. The one that never really counts towards anything. I love it probably more than the "dessert" drink—the coffee I order with Baileys when everyone else chooses some pie or other dessert. I make darn sure, mind you, to order it "on the side" so I can have the Baileys and let the coffee turn cold.

Feeling just great by 6:30 p.m. One beer, one glass of great red wine. Peter has had neither and probably won't think about it until I pour him one with dinner. I feel a nice warm buzz and would never, ever ask for a better buzz feeling than this—if the choice were really mine. How do I feel? Warm, relaxed, soft, creative, content.

Tonight I looked at the smaller wine glasses in our china cabinet. I picked them up and toyed with the idea that I might drink less with them. But, I can just see this highly energetic body of mine flying up and down my stairs to refill the 'lil glass....would be great for the legs and butt but would do nothing for my drinking habit.

So off I go to make a great dinner, be a great wife and mother...and pour myself the drink which is probably the one that takes me to the point where I lose the ability to understand that I shouldn't have another after it.

I love and hate this next drink.

Roberta: Drink in Hand

Glorious night, still sunny and warm, the kids and their pals are playing badminton on the front lawn. I love how their laughter is carried up to the windows, down the hallway and into my office as I work. It's early in the evening, I'm just finishing up *my second vodka cranberry and am feeling absolutely great.*

Light buzz, no commitments tonight, Mike is cooking ribs on the grill and a whole fabulous evening awaits. So many wonderful and fun things to do with this summer night. I'm dying to finish that garden bed in the back yard—should I do that? There's a soft breeze that'll keep the bugs at bay. Or maybe get going on pumping up the new huge inflatable pool I just bought the kids for the back deck…they are so jazzed about it and can hardly wait. It'll provide great relief from tomorrow's heat, plus, this will give me some time with them after a crazy week of work and travel.

Of course, regardless of the activity I select, I will have my drink in hand. I never leave it behind. Ever. Coffee: yes, I find it cold in the bathroom after I put on my makeup. Tea: half-full mugs of it on my bed stand that I return endlessly to the kitchen sink. Water: the ice melts long before I finish it. But that cocktail is my companion in everything I do at night.

Brenda: Missing in Action

Lauren calls from school and asks where I am. My head races trying to figure out what I promised last night. How could I not remember that I told her I'd pick her up from school? She gives me an incredulous sigh. I tell her I'll be right there and as I rush out the door and think back—didn't I have just two or three glasses of wine?

I guess it was enough to make me forget this promise. I know better than to think I'll listen and remember next time. Instead I tell her that she must call me from school any time I promise to pick her up. How can she expect me to remember when

I'm so busy?

Roberta: Rationalizations

I really wish red wine were my drink of choice. Not that I don't absolutely adore a rich Merlot or expensive Cab, but usually only with a meaty meal. Seems to be the only time I have the luxury of not sucking it down fast. And I don't like the cheap stuff, so I probably couldn't afford it as my primary vice, anyway.

But when I'm honest with myself I do find the justification for what I drink interesting—funny these little mind games we play with ourselves.

First of all: I prefer vodka (goes with everything, even the kids' Capri Suns if I'm really desperate for a mixer), whiskey (love Crown Royal, but save it for vacations and outdoor outings due to cost) and occasionally gin (again, prefer the really good stuff, so don't indulge often, and definitely this is a summer drink for me.)

So, vodka it is, but it can get so boring, the same old thing, and here's how I create variety PLUS justify the fact that all those empty calories really aren't so bad:

A) Vodka-orange juice. Number one seller in our household, maybe because it's also what Mike likes best, too. Justification: I am getting a TON of Vitamin C every day, and we all know how good that is for ya. Down side: also getting a TON of calories, and the high sugar content feeds into the craving for more sweets, AKA more drinks

B) Vodka-tomato juice. Hey, this is almost health food. Everyone knows how good tomato-ANYTHING is for you. And can definitely drink this one guilt-free in the morning because...well, I can't really remember why, but I know there's a good reason.

C) Vodka-grapefruit juice. See A.

D) Vodka-cranberry juice. Recent favorite and I'll never have another yeast infection. Down side: gets old fast...can only take tart so long.

E) Vodka-whatever-else is in the fridge/freezer/cabinets/ kids' lunch bag when we're out of all the other stuff. Um...I guess this is when I realize that maybe I've got a little bit of a problem here...

Brenda: When the Cats are Away

The family is now gone on their annual four-day "dad and kids trip". I got up, went on my morning power walk, at first thinking I might skip it until I realized that not only could I pick up some videos, but could also nab a bottle of champagne & OJ. Yes, that drink that is acceptable before noon.

So, now more motivated than ever, I put on my backpack and head off two miles down the street toward the store. The weather is a perfect 70 degrees. As I walk, I remember last year's trip started exactly the same way. The family left and I started in with the champagne. I had to switch to red wine each day at noon that time, too, as I only thought to buy one bottle of champagne on the first day. At the time, I give this no consideration...surely I wouldn't plan to drink at noon! What would that make me? So instead, I buy my one bottle and go about my life.

It is now 12:30 p.m. on the first day and I've already had three glasses. Before this journal entry is finished, I'm sure to have filled the next glass. I'm using the tall, narrow glasses this year, good girl that I am.

For some reason, this year was unlike so many that preceded it. Not sure why exactly. Maybe I've come to that place. That place in time when one knows they must make a change, or that a change is upon them. God knows I've wanted it in the quietest, most intimate places of my being. I feel it sharply, like the shooting pain in my side when I run.

But these come in the morning hours when I first awake and think of the night that shouldn't have been. The morning light that should bring joy, but instead brings with it the guilt and remorsefulness I privately feel for letting myself down yet again. (Later)

So I started with and finished a big bottle of champagne, two glasses of red wine and I take a bottle of Corona to bed with me now for an afternoon nap, and it is Thursday at 4:00 p.m. Never would I have indulged myself with my family here! Oh no, I have so much more self-control than that. I am envied everywhere. It is the talk of the town. How do I stay so thin, so toned, so driven, so successful? Who would ever guess this monkey clings to my back?

I will awake within hours and open a new bottle. Just you wait and see.

Roberta: Day One

Thank God this is almost over. My head is so fuzzy after last night and today I have such an important conference call. I can't wait for this to end and to simply look back at how awful it was.

*I started listening to the hypnotic recording last night,
wow that was something! I went so deep into it. Deeper, deeper,
deeper he'd say, and I thought I would just melt into my bed. I
can't wait to try it again, as I think I was still a little wasted and
finally just fell asleep.*

*Weighed myself this morning, man I've never been that
heavy! Getting ready for a shower...hope I can jerk this slushy
brain of mine into place.*

(Later the same day)

*What an interesting experience this has been already...I
was so sick this morning. Started out really groggy, but thought I'd
feel better after a shower. Within an hour of taking the Topamax
and vitamins though, I was really in bad shape. By noon, I had
vomited a couple of times and had a terrible case of the runs.
Relentless nausea and GI stuff I just don't do very well. Did my
conference call but told everyone I'd come down with something,
and ended up writing off the rest of the day.*

*Decided to drink as much water as possible and go listen
to the hypno CD again, as I couldn't wait to get back to it. It was
great. There's almost a magical quality about it.*

*So what I find most interesting is this: even though I felt
better later in the day, I had absolutely NO desire for a drink.
Typically, when I'm sick, I wait until I'm feeling good enough to
have a drink later...the craving never subsides, so it's a balancing
act of figuring out when my gut can tolerate the liquor. But once
my stomach settled, I decided to make a PBJ on an English
muffin and couldn't think of anything I wanted more than a full
glass of milk! (And despite the empty stomach, I'm not terribly*

hungry, but just wanted to settle it down.)

I'm not sure what to think...has the Topamax already kicked in? Does the hypnotherapy work that fast? Am I going to feel this luxurious lack of craving later tonight, particularly when Mike starts in on the evening cocktails?

So I found myself watching the clock, and I noticed it was 3:30 (which has become my new drinking start time—it's really been concerning me—and my justification has that with my new part-time job, that's when I come home, and naturally that's when cocktail hour should begin, right?) But unlike before, the craving doesn't rear its ugly head.

4:30: Wow, didn't even realize it was 4:30. The only thing I've wanted to drink so far is a ton of water besides that glass of milk I had earlier with the sandwich.

5:30: Surely by now that awful craving will come a calling, but it doesn't—I can hardly believe it.

By the end of the day I felt a lot better (still no craving), the other dosing of vitamins didn't bother my stomach, but I was wiped out and just wanted to get to bed early. Without a drink, woo hoo! Mike and the kids were great...kept it quiet so I could get some shut eye, but it probably wouldn't have mattered, strapped in as I was to my headphones and CD player, going deep, deeper, deeper, ha... My thinking was so much clearer this time, I got into the hypno even better and could see I was really going to enjoy this part of the program. Yikes, a whole new addiction!

Roberta: Day Two

Woke up feeling a lot better, headed to the office and felt like I had this Big Secret. Got a ton of work done, just felt so happy! I guess I was thinking about drinking but only because I didn't want to! Usually the drive home is the drive home to drink—I'm always looking forward to it, and once there, the first order of business is to make a cocktail (gotta "relax", "decompress", "wind down", all that other stuff we always tell ourselves. "Killer day, need a drink.") But I realized that I truly didn't crave one, I was so happy just to sit on the couch and talk with the kids—it was so mundane and wonderful at the same time!

Didn't have anything at all before or with our quick dinner—can't even believe that!

I ended up helping out with Brooke's softball game on a gorgeous sunny night, and the gals played just great. Didn't even have to chew gum, which I often do when I race out of the house and want to hide the smell on my breath. Mike was sitting next to me and I could detect the faint scent of the drink he'd had back home when he got up close. I was reminded of how acutely I could smell tobacco on people after I quit smoking many years ago.

Back home I watched an enjoyably awful chick flick on HBO with Katie and we had a ball making fun of some of the worst acting we'd seen in quite a while. And I STILL didn't want to drink. I only wanted to enjoy this newfound clarity, although I did feel a slight compulsion to get back to that hypno CD in the quiet office bedroom!

By 11:30 or so I started to nod off at the movie's end— could only take so much of that nonsense—and then headed back to my hypnotherapy session, to reinforce this profound change that appears to be taking place in my brain.

Roberta: Day Three

I cannot remember when I felt this good—I am practically euphoric about something most human beings would find positively ordinary: I'm not thinkin' about drinkin'!

I honestly have absolutely no cravings today and am just thrilled. I am surprised to find that I'm hungrier than normal, and seem to want more carbs than usual—maybe as a replacement? I'm usually an egg/meat/cheese eater, but don't seem terribly interested in that today. Don't know why.

And I'm finding a slight "activity void" that is successfully filled by the action of filling glasses with fluids…in my case orange juice, tomato juice, ice water, iced tea, Gatorade and club soda. I know it's more calories and sugar than I probably need, but I'm giving myself permission to eat or drink whatever I truly crave today and will tweak the regimen as I go. I'm assuming it's probably best to go slowly as I make such a significant lifestyle change. I just don't want to get tripped up.

I also became very grouchy mid day…barked at Mike on the phone, snapped at the kids.

I'd been awakened at 3:30 in the morning by the dog, so slept in longer than expected and didn't start on the exercise plan, as intended. But who knows…there are so many changes now. I do think exercise will be an important activity—but again, I'd rather err on the side of taking things slowly at this point.

But the sense of peace, of calm, of freedom from the craving has simply swept me off my feet. Please, God, let this last forever! What fun I had with my kids today after I got over the grouchy stuff. I took Katie to the salon to have her lashes and eyebrows tinted for the first time and the brows were a total disaster. She both laughed and cried at my crude attempts to scrape, scrub and bleach the color off. We spent no less than two hours in the kitchen—much of it right under my beloved liquor cabinet—and I realized later I never once—not ONCE—thought about wanting a drink while we were in there.

Mike came home, made a cocktail, and all I craved was participating in the ritual...bring me something cold in a glass and let's sit down and catch up on our day. I feel normal! Tomorrow I may even have a drink with him to see if one is enough. Is that dangerous? My long-term goal is moderation, not abstinence.

It was so interesting when you called me from the hotel, Brenda. I completely understand how difficult it must be to believe how dramatic these changes are—you'll just have to wait and see for yourself...and you will!

But the image in my mind is so compelling, particularly, as I spent a good part of today under my computer desk, tangled in wires, snorting dust and grouchy as hell—but breaking the bonds of the horrible addiction that has ruled both of our lives. And there you were, with your toned and tanned body wrapped in some gorgeous sarong, sipping a drink on the lanai at an exclusive resort with the people you most treasure...glorious sunset before you, absolute paradise. But you are really in you own private hell because you are completely consumed—as I was only days ago—with getting that next drink, and tomorrow it will be the same for you as it is for millions like us who live with the curse of this addiction.

I cannot wait for you to meet me here on the other side.

Roberta: Day Four

Wild and crazy dreams last night...don't know if it's because of the medication, hypnotherapy, withdrawal, or what! I am such a witch this week—I did not anticipate this level of irritability...today was even worse than yesterday. Honestly, I feel like I'm going to jump out of my skin...again, lashing out at Mike and super sensitive to everything that's going on around me. My Internet search informs me that this is a typical side effect of alcohol withdrawal and so tonight I upped the dose of the Calms Forte. I think it will help.

Tonight I decided to try a glass of wine—I actually find the thought of a vodka cocktail absolutely revolting—it would seem to me like drinking cleaning fluid, which just blows me away, so I'm pretty confident my interest in the wine is clinical, because I want to test the suggestions I've been trying with the hypnotherapy, and I'm dying to know if I have one glass: will I crave another? I haven't been able to stop at one glass in...well, I can't really remember how long.

But last minute evening activities dictated otherwise, so after pouring a very small glass and only taking a couple of sips, and I had to run errands instead.

Later at home I decided to try again—call me crazy, and I swear, this was driven not by craving but complete curiosity. I am not in denial when I tell you I really wanted to know what happens! So I drank half a small (very small) glass while flipping through a magazine, but desired no more and didn't want to push it—by this point it seemed sorta silly, I guess—so I was completely happy to follow up with club soda.

Later, even as I heard Mike make himself a post-golf

game cocktail, I found I didn't want a drink. This is a new pattern that has developed, but continues to amaze me—he comes home and has a drink, and I do not. I mean, this is incredible! The sound of cocktail preparation in the kitchen has always given me full permission to have another drink—regardless of whether or not I may be several drinks ahead—that has somehow been irrelevant in my twisted addicted logic...it would simply be unfair for me to deprive myself when someone else is drinking in my house. I am now ecstatic to learn that this ridiculous rule has somehow been blasted from my healing brain.

So if my wonderfully supportive family can survive the bitchy broad who just moved in, and I can put the brakes on this weird and insatiable appetite that suddenly appeared (I swear, I am eating ALL DAY LONG) I think life will be just about perfect!

Brenda's Darkness Before Dawn

I have to admit, Roberta, I feel both joy and jealousy when I read your e-mails about not wanting to drink, or you not wanting a second drink. I have nothing profound to write tonight. Kinda down that my hypno CDs didn't get here and I have had to put off my start of Topa and vitamins.

I don't get to go have my virgin drink—just another stupid red Merlot, or two or three. Deep down I know that following this weekend is a great way for me to start the program. So sad, the wasted days. I didn't leave the house much, didn't call anyone, didn't want to answer the phone, just watched movies and drank champagne during the day and red wine at night.

Hopefully tomorrow I begin a new journal chapter. I can't wait!

Brenda's First Week

Wow! I love this! To follow up on our phone call today: I had a great evening! Been continuing with the CDs, Topa, and supps, and religiously. Peter went out with his friend to dinner. I had the kids' friends over and Ryan's, too. So I told Lauren I wanted to do my CD (she still thinks they are health & fitness) and would she take everyone to the park for one hour.

My hypnotic suggestions focus on my sipping behavior, my ability to sometimes have just one glass, and I have added: "I often forget about alcohol altogether". That could really be a goal of mine. To consider it an afterthought. Like adding bacon to my green beans... "Yeah, okay, that might taste good tonight!"

I drank sparkling water most the day and night; then I made coffee at around 8 p.m. Then I went for my power walk at 8:30 pm. I didn't even pour myself a glass of wine until I had everyone in bed, a movie on, and my watercolors in front of me at 10 p.m.! I sipped my one glass and just didn't care if I had another or not. Really. So I didn't.

Now, what's so cool about it is this...it was easy. Not a "struggle" with will power or anything like that. Not trying to be good. Is it like this for you? You think to yourself... "Shall I have another glass of wine?" and you answer, "I can if I want to. I'm not breaking any rules if I do." But then you kinda find yourself not doing it, not pouring another. Almost like you have become indifferent. That's how I felt tonight. It was more like a nice thing to wind down with, but I could take or leave the second glass....so

I left it.

Brenda's Continued Success

*I'm at my first party (a prestigious wine tasting event that Peter and I had been planning for weeks), right? And of course, you're supposed to sample beverages all night long. I was paying close attention to my wine consumption, but didn't plan on abstaining—my God, you can't believe how incredible some of that stuff is. So I sipped a glass of champagne, which was great, I drank it slowly. Then the waiter started pouring white wine. I actually completely enjoyed the hand motion and hearing myself say, "No thanks, I'm fine" several times in the night. I was **excited**!*

Through my hypno exercises, I had repeatedly said that I saw myself as being one of the most sober people at any gathering, and sure enough, I was! In fact, for the first time in 21 years, I actually drove us home, as Peter was kinda tipsy. When was the last time that happened?

I was totally sober through the entire party, I remember every minute of every discussion, drove home perfectly, had a great talk with Lauren and her boyfriend when we got home, and didn't pour another glass when we got there, or even think of it.

I also realized how "icky" those who had had too much to drink looked. Yikes. Plus, I ended the night with someone handing me a nice tall wonderful Merlot, and without making it obvious I held it for a while and then just simply set it down and didn't touch it.

This was not work! I drank when I wanted to (moderation!), enjoyed the whole social aspect of it all, but would not go back and change a single part of it. I was monitoring myself on a subconscious level all night with no effort. I did not feel deprived at all and I was totally and utterly in control!

Brenda Forgets to Want it

How could I forget???

Totally forgot to "want" to open a bottle of wine last night. Kimberly fixed me a beautiful Perrier with lemon and it was so refreshing and cold! Not like I had her make that as a replacement for my glass of wine either. She often makes me special drinks that would just sit there, while I carried my wine glass from room to room...never too far from it. I wasn't thinking about anything except fixing dinner when she asked if she could do that for me.

Looking back at last night, this is funny and puzzling. How could I simply just forget about doing something that I used to race home to do each night for the last several years? Then I'd look at the clock: 4 p.m. (damn, too early), 5 p.m. (almost time), 6 p.m. (yeah, drinking hour is here!). And then often 8 p.m. (oops, bottle is empty and nothing to pour in Peter's glass.)

And what will be just as great—and incredible—is that tomorrow is Friday. Used to be my biggest drinking day of the week, too. I know for sure that tomorrow will not seem any different to me than any day this week. Just another wonderful day. Might rent movies...might go out to eat...but with whatever we do it "MAY" include having wine or it may not. But it is not the motivation for wanting Friday to be here. And if we do have wine, I will completely enjoy the smell, the taste, the fun we'll have in choosing a special bottle from our new inventory. And I have a *feeling that I will pour it into our decanter and let it breathe without fear that I'm losing any drinking time!*

And I will "sip" my wine because I am a sipper, not a guzzler. (One of my favorite hypno suggestions.) I sip my wine because that is how one drinks wine—to fully enjoy it for the taste of it—not for the motivation to rush to a buzz and beyond. I have not wanted the noon beer or wine cooler either. Until this very minute I had not thought about my not drinking at lunch! I would often have "something" during the day. How often my kids asked for lunch while were running around and they'd hear me say "No McDonalds...mommy wants a nice salad." When what I really meant was "mommy wants a glass of wine".

How free this feels. And I know that I am just on the first steps of a wonderful journey!

Roberta at Three Weeks

Has it only been three weeks? How in the world can a person be so utterly transformed in just three weeks?

Honestly, I cannot believe this is me, and only now am I beginning to truly fathom that this is no short term, psychosomatically-induced, too-good-to-be-true, temporary change in behavior. Something is happening to this brain. At times I am astonished to think of both how incredible and ordinary I feel. The endless craving is gone. I am in control. I can choose to drink and I can choose not to.

My preference is for one, sometimes two (sometimes no) glasses of wine in the evening or on the weekends. I have no desire to drink hard liquor whatsoever, which boggles my mind. (What a change from my four to five tall glasses of strong vodka cocktails every night.) It takes much longer to finish the wine, as I sip it slowly and enjoy it in a whole new way. I am often surprised to find it later unfinished in the glass.

I am passionately exploring new and wonderful replacement drinks to offset this summer heat: herbal iced teas and coffees, seltzers with lime, or good old fashioned ice water, all of which my kids seem curious about and eager to ask permission to sip. No more "uh uh—that's Mom's drink". What an unexpected and wonderful luxury to be able respond in that way.

So as I launch into week four, I do so with the knowledge that the system is working, it's working well and it's easy to do! I'll be adding the music CDs to the exercise program this week and I picked up an introductory Pilates video to work on some toning.

Other parts of the program are becoming more comfortable and routine, including shaking my vitamin powder into a spicy tomato juice every morning—my favorite take on the Bloody Mary these days—and it seems to make for a perfectly filling breakfast with my newfound lack of appetite. I suppose I should eat more, but I'm just not hungry, as my appetite is apparently hiding out with my alcohol craving. Good riddance to both of them, ha!

I've lost seven pounds so far and am actually looking forward to finally achieving a weight loss goal I thought was out of reach for me. I'd tried so many times, but would inevitably end up backing off on food so I could drink a little more instead, which always perked up my sweet tooth. Vicious cycle.

I anticipate this work week will be a bit more stressful than most, as I have with multiple deadlines, but I approach it all with the knowledge that I have much more mental energy than I did three weeks ago when I was fighting a fuzzy brain, aching eyes and remorseful heart for every night's previous drinking. Life is so good—and I expect it will only get better!

Brenda's Normal Night

Last night I decided to go to the 7 p.m. open swim. Never would I have done this before! How could I when drinking hour started at 6 p.m. and who would ever miss that?

So I drive to the pool and afterwards there is no rush to get home. I stay and talk in the parking lot instead! I would never have done that before…in the back of my mind, I knew that wine was waiting at home.

Then I get home and decide to cook a great late dinner. No kids tonight so I set a nice table outside in the courtyard. Not once do I make a motion to the wine cabinet. I know that I don't want any before dinner. I want to have it with dinner for the same reason I wouldn't eat a baked potato before my dinner!

So, I put some wonderful music on, and prepare the steaks on the grill, the garlic and olive tossed peppers, etc. Lastly, I set a nice bottle of Merlot out with two crystal glasses (my smallest ones.) When Peter gets home, he smiles as he sees that we will have this romantic dinner alone. He opens the wine and pours two glasses and carries them to the table for us. We enjoy our dinner and sip our first glasses. After dinner is over, we go into the family room to watch a favorite TV show. He asks how my wine is and I completely enjoy saying "I'm fine right now". I mean I **completely** *enjoy hearing these words come out of my mouth because I really feel fine and content.*

Then later that night, he pours two more glasses for us. I no longer hold my glass or feel the need to keep it right by me. I take the rest of the night to sip my second glass.

Just a fantastic night! Then to top it off, I wake up feeling great and am ready to go do my power walk. I LOVE feeling this good every morning. Long gone is the heavy, guilty head that can't do much in the morning but berate myself.

This is a beautiful thing!

Brenda Sums up an Incredible Journey

How incredible this journey has become. Never have I experienced anything like it and I've had some incredible highs in my life. My business ventures have created times of pure satisfaction...but this is different. My personal fitness goals have been a very positive thing in my life...but this is different. My family life is one of great joy...but this is different.

This is the easiest-best thing I've ever done. Yeah, that's it. The best thing that I have done that has been this easy. My business ventures took a lot of hard work. Totally consumed me 24/7. My fitness goals came from many hours of sweat. My family life is one of daily effort to be a great wife and loving mother; it is wonderful and natural, but an effort nonetheless.

The success of gaining control over my drinking has been so easy. Okay, I have been diligent in taking my supplements and meds, listening to my hypno CDs and walking. But the return on my investment has been so significant! The script written in my hypnosis totally defines me now. It feels as though it became who I was the minute I heard it for the first time. And it is reinforced with every morning sun.

I enjoy every opportunity that is presented—drinking wine with dinner, not drinking with dinner, enjoying a couple of glasses of wine with my best friend, ordering iced tea with lunch on a Saturday afternoon. Sadly, every opportunity used to be one that I tried and often succeeded in fitting alcohol around. I accept that alcohol does have a small place in my life, as does butter! But it doesn't control me, harm me, or make me regret its use.

I went into this with eyes and heart wide open. I wanted desperately to change. And I would have been willing to work hard to get to this incredible place I now find myself. I would have paid anything for it. But it has all been so wonderfully easy. The desire to change was the catalyst.

And this program was the answer.

Author's Note: It can be immensely helpful to find someone with whom to communicate and who is starting this journey the same time as you, even a new online friend, who you may wish to email privately. Visit the discussion board at www.mywayout.org for more information.

CHAPTER **THREE**

It is a mistake to try to look too far ahead.
The chain of destiny can only be grasped
one link at a time.
—Winston Churchill

POTENTIAL SIDE EFFECTS

his program is highly effective and has the potential to change your life, plain and simple. But before you get started, you should know as much about each aspect of it as possible, including what to expect in the way of side effects, particularly from topiramate. Again, I hope you can benefit from the personal experiences of those who have gone before you, so I am sharing what I observed in my own case, as well as what I have learned from others.

And I also will say again: do not attempt this program unless you work closely with a physician. Taking any drug—even aspirin—affects some people differently than the vast majority of those who use it without any trouble. Your doctor must be involved, and you must tell her or him how you are faring if you decide to include topiramate in your program to get control of your drinking.

I am aware of some individuals who, for one reason

or another, simply opted out of taking the medication but followed the rest of the program, and still seemed to enjoy success. My personal experience indicates the benefit of topiramate far outweighs any short-term side effects. It is a powerfully effective agent that simultaneously targets two neurotransmitter pathways in the brain resulting in a reduced craving for alcohol. Until formal studies are done, I feel more comfortable supporting a fully integrative program. But given a choice of eliminating the medication or not doing the program at all, obviously, opt for taking a pass on topiramate, and follow the rest of the program.

Which brings me back to the side effects. Frankly, until now, I've been somewhat surprised at the limited information many patients—at least those taking the drug for other reasons—have received from their physicians about some of the symptoms that may arise from topiramate. The side effects typically are temporary, but can be somewhat startling if they appear without the patient being advised beforehand.

And it is reassuring to know that the University of Texas researchers reported "no serious adverse events" when the drug was used for alcohol treatment in their clinical trial; only five of 75 participants withdrew from the study because of problems from the medication. According to them, these adverse effects reportedly included: dizziness: 28%; paraesthesia (a burning or prickling sensation in the hands, arms, legs or feet): 57.3%; psychomotor slowing: 26.7%; memory or concentration impairment:

18.7%; and weight loss: 54.7%.[1]

While short-lived, I found the cognitive impairment associated with the drug to be the most interesting aspect of the program—and, again, it's one of the reasons the other therapies play such an important role, as I believe they can help offset at least some of the side effects. Several weeks into the program, I discovered a nootropic agent (basically, a "smart pill") that very much helped mitigate the problem—and interestingly, it further accelerated my weight loss, which I'll get to later.

I would never, ever, have traded this experience for anything in the world, as it gave me my life back, but I was enormously grateful for the topiramate discussion boards I discovered on the Internet. A good sense of humor helped, too, because it augmented the information I gleaned online and helped me a lot those first few weeks.

While others complained of ills like tingling fingers, lethargy or anxiety, my sharpest showdown with side effects was the "topa dopa effect," and for a few weeks I kept a somewhat low profile in my dim-witted cognitive fog.

Here are some of my experiences during that period: I occasionally found myself substituting incorrect words in my speech. For this reason, I decided to hold off on public speaking engagements, at least until I was able to rev up my mental faculties with the new supplement. It helped tremendously, because once the topiramate had

---

[1] *Johnson BA, Ait-Daoud N, Bowden CL, DiClemente CC, Roache JD, Lawson K, Javors MA, Ma JZ. Oral topiramate for treatment of alcohol dependence; a randomized controlled trial. Lancet 2003; 361 (9370): 1677-1685.*

taken up residence in my brain, even simple phone calls could trip me up. I remember once contacting my supervisor, an easy going, but religiously devout man, to inform him that I needed to cancel our apartment (appointment).

At home, my family learned to laugh at mom's quirky new behavior, so my husband would simply roll his eyes when I'd tell him that I didn't want the younger kids to see him smoking that expensive new Cuban *guitar*, or ask him to stop at the store to pick up some extra virgin *foreign* oil for the vinaigrette dressing I was making.

And forget about keeping the kids' names straight.

Actually, the word substitution was not nearly as embarrassing as the other odd problem that seemed to crop up occasionally: drawing a complete and utter mental blank when attempting to recall words, compute math, or perform a number of other menial mental tasks. It's as if the spigot was abruptly shut off.

For instance, I once had to ask my ten year old for the name of the espresso bar we had visited as I tried to write a check, wedged as we were in front of the line of several pierced, tattooed and obviously irritated customers. This was no fly-by-night operation, and I was surrounded by all the obvious clues—but no storefront sign from my vantage point.

In a moment of sheer desperation, I finally leaned over to my daughter, pretended to cough, and whispered, "What's this place called?" I shrank in embarrassment as she responded loudly "We're at Starbucks, Mom!"

I think the medication must temporarily exacerbate pre-existing deficits. For instance, while I am, quite frankly, highly demanded for my professional skills, I have never had any sort of intellectual capacity for visuospatial thinking. As a result, I am a complete idiot on the road. Or in a new city, a large building, a small building, or someone's home. You put me there, I'll get lost.

I don't know that others in the program suffered to the same degree, but I found driving particularly challenging, especially when I was dosing up. I never, ever felt as though I lost my ability to control my vehicle or make good judgement calls—that's not it at all. But at times, at least early on, I'd simply lose track momentarily of where I was going or how to get there.

In fact, I joked with my husband at one point that I might need to install a GPS in my car to help get me to my office, which was a mere ten-minute, direct drive from our house.

Getting home was equally challenging. My teen-age daughter reminded me as I occasionally drove first past our street, then past our house—where we have lived for seven years—to back up and try again. I learned to allow a generous margin of time when finding new locations (houses for parties, offices for business stops, etc.,) as there was no way I'd make it in time otherwise.

Again, I think my symptoms probably were more exaggerated than they would be for most people, although I have read a few cases of driving confusion. But like the other frustrations caused by the medication, it was short-lived, so I tried to see the humor in it and trusted others who assured me the symptoms would pass. They did, quite painlessly.

As I wrote earlier, I'm not ashamed to admit my problems with alcohol, because I was genetically disposed to it. But I am ashamed that before I quit drinking to excess, I'd sometimes run errands or drive home from social events after drinking more than I should have (clearly much more dangerous than any side effects of the medication) even though I never did so when I was terribly impaired, and somehow had the good fortune of never being in an accident or stopped and given a breathalyzer test.

Yet despite my casual approach and strong feelings to the contrary about drinking and driving (at least while I was thinking about it when sober) I harbored a secret, paralyzing fear that I would be pulled over and arrested, which I was reminded of on a daily basis when I read the names of those who landed in the DUI log of our newspaper.

I visualized my name alongside theirs, given my many years of drinking and our state's rigorous drunk driving laws. It seemed inevitable and terrifying to me that my name would appear in that column one day. How would I face my family, my friends, my peers, and the civic groups with whom I worked?

So to be rid of this secret fear was an incredible relief—but it was ironic to find myself with a new driving concern. At one point, I could hardly find my way to work and wondered if my headlight were out or my license expired and if I *were* stopped by the police, how would I explain where I was going? But at least I knew I would be able to pass the field sobriety test, and not land in that dreaded section of the newspaper the following day!

The other dramatic—but positive—side effect I experienced from topiramate was weight loss, which is quite common, and in fact the medication is often prescribed (again, off-label) for binge eating and obesity because of its powerful ability to suppress the appetite. While not effective for every patient, most who take topiramate find their appetites significantly diminished, and physicians report their patients lose 15% to 20% of body weight.

I lost nearly 30 pounds in about three months, but had also begun taking the nootropic supplement, which had its own anorectic, or appetite suppressant qualities, so my caloric intake had become significantly reduced. I limited my small meals to healthy choices. Like others, I found any desire for greasy junk food virtually disappeared, and was replaced with a yen for salads, protein, and small portions of carbohydrates. For the first time in my life, I also lost the desire to top off dinner with dessert. I can say without reservation it was the most painless diet I had ever undertaken.

Those of us who use topiramate to help control our drinking have an added benefit over others who use the medication strictly for weight loss: our appetites are reduced *and* we no longer desire or consume those hundreds of empty alcohol calories each week. You will be astounded by what a tremendous difference it makes.

For example, I used to easily drink three to five cocktails each evening (and more on weekends). They were usually vodka drinks with some form of juice, and I recently calculated that since I made them strong and in tall glasses, each drink was loaded with at least 300 calories. Once I started the program, I realized I had walked away from thousands of calories each week I had previously consumed on a daily basis. Frankly, I'm surprised I wasn't the size of barn by my early 40's. No wonder the weight seemed to melt away!

Physicians report higher doses of topiramate generally result in more weight loss and in addition to being painless, patients tend to come to a new weight and then stabilize. In terms of dieting, it's a relief to know this is not yet another "yo-yo" plan. I had gone that route in years past, so I waited months before finally donating or altering the many clothes in my wardrobe that no longer fit, or buying outfits in my new smaller size.

To this day, I find myself in the dressing room trying on pants or skirts that are much too large and returning to the rack for the next size down—it's still hard to believe that this new body belongs to me. And it's almost impossible to comprehend that the weight that had dropped off so easily would be a permanent change, but in fact, it is. Most people my age worry about their waistlines getting larger;

I am celebrating my new lean appearance, and have no worries about regaining the weight I lost.

Incidentally, although I've not read this in any of the literature, I've noted a number of individuals asking if topiramate increases one's metabolism, because as I understand, some folks actually consume the same amount of calories while taking it without gaining weight. Again, I've seen no medical evidence to support this, but simply mention it in the event you notice the same effect and do not wish to lose weight, and I encourage you to remember to keep an eye on the scale and adjust your diet appropriately.

A commonly reported side effect of the topiramate you'll want to be prepared for is tingling of the extremities. One woman in my program said she actually enjoyed the sensation (we joked mischievously once that it would be nice to have more control over where the tingling occurred). I think most people find it simply annoying, as we all do when an arm or leg "falls asleep." I found it much less bothersome than others, and like most side effects, this one eventually passed.

One of the more bizarre side effects I observed—and many others experienced—is the onset of a metallic taste when drinking carbonated sodas or other canned beverages. My family rarely drinks soda, and the bottled water we consume usually comes in the plastic or glass containers, so it wasn't until I happened to purchase an aluminum six-pack of seltzer water one day I understood what the hubbub on the discussion boards was about. What an awful taste! It reminded me of putting galvanized nails in my mouth as a child when playing "carpenter"—truly awful.

For those who live on diet sodas or any other carbonated beverages, prepare yourself, because you'll probably not want to get near the stuff, at least until this particular phase passes.

The side effects mentioned above describe my personal experience and those of the individuals with whom I've worked closely, but it's worth noting again that medications can affect everyone differently.

The Internet provided a wealth of information and I collected everything I could before undertaking this endeavor, because I knew the topiramate would be an important therapy in my program. It was incredibly helpful to read accounts tying personal experiences to side effects, but you can imagine my concern as I learned about those side effects that were never described in the medical literature or clinical trials by patients taking it for bipolar, migraines, binge eating, and obsessive-compulsive disorder. Curiosity evolved to downright concern as I imagined myself stricken with the same afflictions I read about: depression, insomnia, and hair thinning! Honestly, I wondered at one point if I should just stick to drinking. (Thankfully, none of the side effects came to pass, and in all fairness, many of the patients whose postings I read were taking other meds at the same time.)

Again, it's impossible to predict how this medication will affect you, and it's something you'll want to discuss with your doctor if you make the decision to try this plan.

I am absolutely convinced, as are others who have found success with this program, that the nutritional supplements, hypnotherapy sessions, and simple exercise will help prevent many of the side effects described by those who take the medication on its own. I was meticulous in considering potential side effects—and how to address each of them—when developing the vitamin regimen.

For instance, Vitamin B12, folic acid and potassium can all help minimize the tingling effect. Zinc, magnesium, selenium and biotin may prevent potential hair thinning. (My hair actually looked *better* once I started the program.) The hypnotherapy itself can be customized to reduce a number of unwanted side effects you may otherwise experience. And the simple 15-20 minute exercise program three times a week will energize your body and brain to help combat the fatigue, cognitive slowing, anxiety or insomnia that others may notice when taking the medication alone.

From my experience, the most commonly reported side effects—both good and bad—have been: weight loss, cognitive slowing, fatigue, anxiety, tingling, and a metallic taste in one's mouth. I would say participants in the program average three or so of the symptoms (with weight loss counted as one) and more often than not, they are short-lived. The appetite suppression tends to remain.

Although unusual, the most serious reported potential side effects are kidney stones (1.5%) or, again rarely, a form of glaucoma usually resolved by discontinuing the medication. (Symptoms typically occur within the first month.) Drinking large amounts of water, as is recommend in this program, should help prevent the former, and diligence in monitoring vision changes—and seeking out a doctor immediately should you notice any ocular disturbances, such as blurry vision or pain—can help you avoid eye problems. More recently, Ortho-McNeil has notified physicians and updated its product labeling to include information about "nonanion gap acidosis", a decrease in electrolyte levels, that can be detected by a blood test. Symptoms may include an increased rate of breathing or irregular heartbeat. Decreased sweating or increased body temperature are rare but important conditions to watch for, as well.

While some of this discussion about possible side effects may concern you, I simply want to be honest and thorough about what you may experience, what clinical trials have demonstrated, and what's included on the medicine's product packaging regarding potential side effects. Again, undertake the program only with commitment, common sense and consultation with a doctor. You need to report any unusual symptoms so they can be observed and addressed.

In my experience, patients tell their physicians they find the temporary side effects, if any, a small price to pay for the overwhelming transformation that takes place when the craving to drink excessively disappears and they regain control of their lives, relationships, future, and dignity.

CHAPTER **FOUR**

> *What lies behind us and what lies before us
> are tiny matters compared to what lies
> within us.*
> —*Ralph Waldo Emerson*

THE PROGRAM

*Y*ou will find this program easy to follow and you may be surprised at just how quickly your craving fades away. It works equally well for binge drinkers, who have reported to me an improvement in their ability to drink responsibly when placing themselves in social situations that formerly got them into trouble. It's not magic—don't get me wrong—we all need to work at this in our own way, but I truly believe this program makes our goals more achievable, with a greater chance for long-term success than other therapies many of us have considered or tried.

The program includes four steps:

1) Six weeks of a combined vitamin, mineral, amino acid, and herb therapy, formulated specifically to address detoxification and craving reduction;

2) One month of powerfully effective daily behavior

modification hypnotherapy sessions, all done in the privacy of your own home;

3) Twelve weeks (or longer) of topiramate administration; and

4) A light exercise program of 15 to 20 minutes three times a week

Modifications in your diet will also ensure your success, and because the recommendations are simple and straightforward, they require no major alterations in your menu planning.

The program, will, however, dramatically change your life in the most positive and fundamental way.

At the end of the six-week period, your vitamin menu is drastically reduced to drinking the nutritional powder—usually with breakfast—that is already included in the program and is easy to find in most grocery store health food sections or online. It contains a well-balanced mix of vitamins, minerals, and amino acids, the latter of which is particularly effective in your lifetime maintenance plan of craving reduction.

You will take topiramate for 12 weeks—or longer. *This is an individual decision and must be made between you and your physician.* Just as a diabetic requires insulin, some patients feel they can best maintain the delicate biochemical balance their bodies require with ongoing pharmacological support. Your doctor may continue to prescribe topirmate or consider transitioning you to other anti-craving medications as they become available. Some individuals find the combination of nutritional supplements and hypnotherapy sufficient tools to help them stay the course. Successful patients are diligent about incorporating both into their lives regularly.

A continued program of light exercise and healthy diet will support your permanent goal of moderation or abstinence—you must determine your goal beforehand—and like those who have gone before you, you will probably lose weight as you gain control over your addiction.

Again, please keep the weight loss factor in mind if it would be detrimental for you to lose a significant amount of body mass. I relished this aspect of the program myself, and as mentioned earlier, one of the supplements I used to ward off the potential and temporary cognitive effects of topiramate further accelerated my weight loss. (But that particular supplement is optional.)

I found the demands of my work required a temporary bump in mental function until my brain adjusted to the medication, so the supplement—Adrafinil, or Olmifon®—helped immensely. I was fine once I got through this phase, and discontinued its use after several weeks.

Another powerful and exciting tool you will have at your disposal, and for the rest of your life, is the hypnotherapy system included in this program, which you will use conveniently in your home, and which you will learn to easily customize to your individual needs. You may be astonished to find out just how effective and truly life transforming this piece of the therapeutic program is. And best of all, after the initial month or so of regular use—or longer if you wish—it will always be available to you, should you need a "tune-up" down the road.

What follows is information about all of the components that make up this program, so you have a fundamental understanding about each of them before you put them to work for you. It's important to remember—vital in fact—that while each of them are critical, *it is imperative they are undertaken together* because you simply will not achieve the same level of success others have enjoyed unless you adopt a comprehensive approach. Clearly, the attitude of many—and admittedly, I was once one of them—is to pop a pill and make the problem go away.

I promise you, it doesn't work like that.

Part One: Topiramate

Topiramate, manufactured by Ortho-McNeil Pharmaceutical, and marketed as Topamax® by Johnson and Johnson, has been used safely and effectively for nearly a decade as an anticonvulsant medication to treat epileptic seizures. It is a derivative of the naturally occurring sugar monosaccharide D-fructose.

For drinkers, topiramate works by washing away excessive dopamine in the brain, which both reduces the pleasurable effects of alcohol and eliminates craving. There is compelling evidence to indicate it has the same positive results for those affected by other addictive behaviors and interesting trials are underway to test its efficacy for smokers and individuals suffering from cocaine addiction, obsessive compulsive disorder, and even kleptomania. It seems to have a pronounced effect on the brain's reward signaling system.

To date, few pharmacological agents have been proven effective against the battle of the bottle, and while researchers assume they may never fashion a pill to completely cure any form of addiction, they have long sought a medication to help people diminish or eliminate their alcohol problem. At the time of this writing, there are three medications approved in the US for alcoholics: Antabuse®, naltrexone (trade name Revia®), and acamprosate (Campral®).

Antabuse® doesn't reduce craving, but instead makes drinkers sick once they consume alcohol. Naltrexone, which has been proven to reduce cravings once a person has already quit drinking, has not been shown as clinically effective as topiramate—at least when used on its own. And acamprosate, the most recently FDA approved medication, is shown to reduce the desire to drink, but can only be taken by those who have quit drinking completely.

The public learned about topiramate's off-label use for alcohol addiction in the spring of 2003 when the results of a clinical trial were reported in the prestigious medical journal *The Lancet* and national headlines followed. Led by Professor Bankole A. Johnson, M.D., Ph.D., and his San Antonio research team at South Texas Addiction Re-

search and Technology (START) Center, the study generated great excitement because topiramate not only promoted abstinence, but was also the first anti-craving
medication that could be initiated while participants were
beginning to curtail their drinking. (Since then, Professor
Johnson has been appointed Chairman of the Department
of Psychiatric Medicine at the University of Virginia.)

According to the institute's press release, the medication "has the capacity to ameliorate the turbulence of anxiety and mood instability that accompanies cessation from
alcohol" and "produced a robust effect on improving maintenance of abstinence and reduced alcohol use." The statement concluded, "A single pharmacologic agent that
enhances early abstinence, stabilizes mood and anxiety
symptoms, and promotes long-term abstinence with only
modest psychosocial intervention is indeed a remarkable
treatment advance."[2]

The evidence was certainly compelling. All 150 patients enrolled in the initial clinical trial were drinking
heavily (defined as at least five standard drinks daily for
men or at least three for women) when they began and
were then randomized to receive topiramate or a placebo
for three months with minimum intervention behavioral
treatment therapy sessions. The START Center patients
taking topiramate were six times more likely than those
who received the placebo to continue to abstain for one

[2] Robert Malcolm, quoted in The University of Texas Health Science Center at San Antonio
"Seizure drug improves abstinence from drinking, study shows", press release, 15 May 2003,
<http://www.uthscsa.edu/STARTcenter/topiramatePR.pdf >

month during the three-month trial, while those taking the placebo were four times more likely to drink heavily for an entire month during the trial.

Other conclusions demonstrated the following:

- After three months, 13 out of the 55 topiramate-taking participants who completed the trial, or 24 percent, had abstained continuously for a month. Only two out of 48 in the placebo group, or four percent, had a month sober.

- In the topiramate group, 28 out of 55, or 51 percent, did not binge for a month-long period, compared with eight out of 48, or 17 percent, of those taking the placebo. Those taking the drug were nearly four times less likely to binge.

- At the end of the study, placebo recipients reported more than twice as much craving as those in the topiramate group.[3]

Johnson and his team are clear leaders in the "neuropsychopharmacology" of addiction and have since identified discrete drinking subtypes, as well as evaluation protocols and treatment recommendations for each. Johnson theorizes that alcohol-dependent individuals are classified as fundamentally early or late onset drinkers. The characteristics of both are determined largely in part by their genetic makeup, he claims, with the early onset type

[3] *Johnson BA, Ait-Daoud N, Bowden CL, DiClemente CC, Roache JD, Lawson K, Javors MA, Ma JZ. Oral topiramate for treatment of alcohol dependence; a randomized controlled trial. Lancet 2003; 361 (9370): 1677-1685.*

generally starting as impulsive drinkers, and the second group usually beginning in response to adult stressor factors such as work or child rearing.

According to Johnson, medications must be tailored to each drinker type's brain chemistry. That is why, at the time of this writing, he believes topiramate is appropriate for all (including late onset) drinkers, and is involved in studies using a combination of Zofran® (ondansetron), an anti-nausea drug, and naltrexone for early onset drinkers.

Ultimately, Johnson hopes to develop a simple genetic test and, using it alongside the Positron Emission Tomography (PET imaging scans) he currently employs to evaluate the brain composition of alcoholics, believes he can effectively match the best specific pharmacological treatment plan tailored to individual patient needs.

With all the exciting advances in psychopharmacology, we may soon learn that some new medication or drug cocktail will oust topiramate as king of the hill in balancing brain chemistry. In fact, acamprosate, which was approved by the FDA in July 2004, may be a contender for those who select abstinence. We will simply have to await the comparative data.

But for our purposes, it doesn't really matter, because it's only one piece—albeit a very important one—of gaining control over the problem, and to date topiramate has been proven more effective than anything else for those who are drinking when they begin an alcohol cessation program. If, one day, something better comes along, with clinical evidence to support it, a simple substitution in this program is easy to accommodate. The other components, however, have stood the test of time.

To avoid harsh side effects, topiramate must be administered carefully in terms of dosing, which means starting with a low dose (typically a 25 mg. tablet the first week) and tapering up slowly. Those who are sensitive to medications may need to split the pill or start with the "sprinkle" capsule, which is about half the strength and can be mixed with food.

Also, once you are up to the 50 mg. dose and higher, it's important that topiramate be taken twice a day rather than administering the day's full dosage at once. Refer to Chapter Five and the dose escalation chart found there.

Part Two: Nutritional Supplements

Many recovery books on the market claim that taking the proper combination of nutritional supplements will end your addiction to alcohol by replacing key chemicals your body lacks, thus eliminating cravings. I know this because I bought the books, tried the plans, and really, really wanted them to work. They didn't. One of them had nearly four dozen vitamins and minerals listed that I was instructed to purchase—some of which I simply could not find or buy in the proper doses.

After that experience I wondered if a visit to a posh outpatient treatment facility might be a more reasonable option. That way, I could simply allow someone else to handle the complex formulas, endless vitamin administration, and strict food menu planning. If I had to do all that myself, it seemed I would have time for little else in my life.

Don't misunderstand me: I knew the books I read were fundamentally right about the value of nutrients, and nobody is a stronger proponent of nutritional supplements than I. I've been researching vitamins, minerals, and amino acids for two decades and I understand how critical they are to the success of an alcohol recovery program.

But we are all busy people. We need a program that is reasonable and fits our lifestyle, and none of the books I read fit mine.

Vitamins and supplements aren't a cure, but if taken in the proper combination, they are a powerful means to overcome your craving for alcohol and will support you during the inevitable withdrawal process as you begin your road to recovery.

Withdrawal is a very important consideration. Even though early to middle stage drinkers may not suffer full blown DTs, you can be sure your central nervous system will undergo extreme agitation when its blood alcohol level drops.

Symptoms may include irritability, anxiety, nausea, nervousness, and insomnia. You're going to need something to help with this transition, and you'll find it in the combination of vitamins, supplements, amino acids, herb extracts and homeopathic offerings.

Late stage drinkers may need more intensive intervention, and there are medications to assist with the transition. Talk with your health care provider about this if you feel you are in need of additional support.

All the other elements in the program will help you, but you absolutely must heal and prepare your body as you undertake this effort. Consider—even visualize—that the supplements you are about to introduce into your system are your own personal team of microscopic housekeepers, personal trainers, therapists and nutritionists, all of whom are about to set up residence on your property, and they're going to clean up shop!

Now let's walk through the menu of nutrients that can help you reach your goal, and don't let the long and hard-to-pronounce names of some of these supplements intimidate you. They may be tongue twisters, but they will reduce both the effects of withdrawal and the powerful craving to return to heavy alcohol use.

Heavy drinkers almost always are deficient in a number of nutrients, such as Vitamins B and C, as well as minerals like magnesium, chromium and zinc. Boosting your system with supplements such as generous doses of Vitamin C will help strengthen your body, cleansing the tissues of excessive alcohol and reducing your withdrawal symptoms in the process.

Other nutrients critical to the plan include the B-complex vitamins, amino acids such as L-glutamine, and the herb extracted from kudzu root, all of which are powerful anti-craving agents. Evening Primrose Oil provides the very important fatty acid GLA (gamma-linolenic acid) which stimulates production of prostaglandin E, a brain chemical that plays a role in preventing withdrawal symptoms and depression. Milk thistle, which is commonly recommended to aid the liver and counteract the harmful effects of alcohol, has been reported to actually regenerate injured liver cells.

Another deficiency often found in drinkers is Vitamin B3. Researchers have observed many alcoholics spontaneously stop drinking when they began taking niacin supplements (niacin is a form of Vitamin B3) and have concluded there is a relationship between niacin deficiency and alcohol addiction. In fact, Bill Watson, the co-founder of Alcoholics Anonymous, was himself a strong proponent of niacin therapy among alcoholics and believed it helped with craving reduction.

Years of research conducted on brain neurotransmitters reveals the interesting role of amino acids. They are the precursors to neurotransmitters, the chemicals that allow nerve cells to pass messages to one another. Early animal research indicated the amino acid L-glutamine promoted reduced alcohol intake when used as an isolated supplement.

In follow up double blind human studies alcoholics treated with D,L-phenylalanine, L-tyrosine, L-glutamine, and L-tryptophan, plus a multi-vitamin and mineral supplement, enjoyed significant reduction in withdrawal symptoms and craving compared to those who took a placebo. They also suffered less stress than individuals in a control group.

Additional research has provided compelling evidence that amino acids play an important role in brain function, including findings that D,L-phenylaline and L-tyrosine both increase levels of norepinepherine in the brain, thus improving mood; L-glutamine curbs the desire for alcohol and sugar; and L-tryptophan increases brain levels of serotonin, which reduces depression, anxiety, and stress.

Amino acid supplementation is recognized as a safe and effective therapy for problem drinkers, particularly those who find themselves stressed, depressed or fatigued, and that's why it plays such a critical role in this program.

Part Three: Hypnotherapy

Hypnosis—or more accurately—self-hypnosis, relaxation, visualization, meditation, and positive affirmations— are all integrated into this powerful and highly effective behavior modification program. They will provide dramatic results, *if you are motivated and follow them as instructed*. I can't say enough about how crucial personal motivation is. No one else can do this for you, wish it for you, or make it happen for you. And you can't put it off, either. If you feel silly, nervous or apprehensive about hypnotherapy, the time to get over it is now.

Hypnosis and the associated techniques work because they allow you to open up your subconscious mind, remove old, unhealthy or unwanted patterns or behaviors and replace them with new desirable ones. Once your conscious mind taps into the incredibly powerful and influential subconscious, the area where your beliefs are stored and your behaviors controlled, almost anything is possible.

I would not have comprehended, nor promoted, the unparalleled power of the subconscious mind had I not lived this experience myself, and in fact, I have used the same techniques when helping friends adapt these behavior modification exercises to achieve other goals. The mind is incredibly complex and strong, and the subconscious simply waits to hear from you when and if you're ready to make positive changes.

These changes, however, require complete relaxation, intense focus, and a closing of the conscious mind, so the subconscious may be opened, released and unlocked. It doesn't happen by itself, and it's why you need tools and instructions for the self-directed steps to take you there. But once you discover them, they're yours for life, and you will find them invaluable. Self-hypnosis, and the hypnotic suggestions that result, will transform you.

As an overview, the CDs in this program will prepare and then guide you to a desired level of relaxation and eventually bring you into a deep hypnotic state. You are in control of whatever level you want to reach. Once there, you are provided with information than can permanently motivate you to overcome your reliance on alcohol.

At an appropriate point, you are also directed to insert you own positive suggestions and messages into your subconscious. It's as if you've suddenly become a wonderfully proficient software programmer with an unlimited capacity to create whatever application you wish.

While many drinkers share common behaviors, we are all individuals with our own personal issues, so this is an unparalleled opportunity to customize a program for specific needs, which is remarkably unique. For instance, you'll be asked beforehand to think about the cues that typically remind you that you want a drink. Is it the sound of ice cubes clinking into a glass when your partner makes a cocktail? The urge to put yourself in a dangerous bingeing situation when a particular person calls to invite you out? The liquor billboard you pass by on the freeway every single weekday?

Believe it or not, you can "trick" your mind into turning those negative cues into positive, post-hypnotic affirmations by programming it to do so when you're in the deep hypnotic and suggestive state. The sound of ice cubes will soon become an automatic desire for a glass of cold, refreshing water. Your friend's phone call can change to become a reminder to spend a fun evening with one of the kids doing something special. The billboard is now a daily reaffirmation—one that grows stronger every time you pass it—that you have met and succeeded in your goal of gaining control over your drinking.

You will plant these images and thoughts in your mind during this initial 30-day period until the concepts become your new reality.

Sound goofy? It isn't. It's powerful stuff. It certainly helped me understand how dozens of audience members could behave in such a bizarre manner at those highly entertaining hypnosis shows and how, with limited motivation and only minutes of hypnotic suggestion, would embarrass themselves in front of hundreds of strangers.

So it shouldn't come as any surprise that someone who greatly desires change in his or her life and is committed to using a quality program that incorporates other powerful behavioral techniques—as well as the integrative elements in this entire therapeutic program—is practically assured of success. And the best thing about the hypnosis component of this program is that there is no audience; it's just between you and yourself.

Part Four: Exercise

Don't be put off by what may appear on the surface to be a mundane mandate. You're about to be so rejuvenated in both body and spirit, you will find this part of the program worth fitting into your schedule.

And remember those personalized hypnotic cues I mentioned? Feel free to drop a few in about exercise if you need some additional motivation. I literally found myself up and in my running gear at 6:30 one morning, exuberant dog at my side, before I realized I'd re-set my alarm clock allowing me to sleep in, as a noisy truck had awakened me in the middle of the night and I'd been unable to get back to sleep.

It wasn't until a few minutes later when I was somewhat coherent and practically out the door I remembered I'd included a hypnotic suggestion in the previous evening's session about looking forward to a morning run (and I don't even like to run, truth be told.)

But neither my bossy subconscious—nor my dog— was going to let me off the hook by then, so away I went. It was great way to start the day.

The important role of exercise in one's life is obvious; it clearly has a positive affect on cardiovascular health, emotional fitness, weight maintenance, and the list goes on. But compelling new evidence points to a direct link between aerobic exercise and craving reduction in alcohol dependent individuals, as well.

In a study funded by the National Institute on Drug Abuse and National Institute on Alcohol Abuse and Alcoholism, researchers focused on the production of endorphins generated by aerobic exercise and concluded they are critical in helping reduce alcohol cravings.

Exercise offered other benefits, as well, including creating a sense of well being, gaining control over one's environment, learning new skills, developing self-esteem, and filling the time formerly spent drinking in a constructive new way.

Participants in the study worked out in three 15-minute gym sessions the first week, building to four 20-minute sessions, and the pilot group found they not only stayed sober, but enjoyed better health and a new lust for life. [4]

I strongly favor an exercise program that is reasonable, realistic and sustainable, so I recommend you not go out and buy expensive equipment that will end up in next year's garage sale, purchase a membership to a health club that will go unused, or buy a series of workout videos for which you are not well suited. We're talking about long-term commitment here, and you need something you'll stick with. Some of the most effective activities may be right out your front door at a community swimming pool. In fact, researchers have found that swimming and exercise to music are the best way to release endorphins.

I always envied swimmers, but never took to the water myself. And again, I don't particularly enjoy running, but did purchase a treadmill when I began this program, so I could use it inside during inclement weather, and I walked briskly outdoors three times a week whenever possible. I found using a CD player with recordings of upbeat music—in fact I even selected songs with positive and supportive messages to reinforce my goals—was something I practically looked forward to on many days. And it was reinforced every time I stepped on the scale.

At times for a change of pace, and when alone at home, I would draw the curtains closed, crank up those same songs on the stereo, and dance like a crazy woman in

[4]*Northeast Network Healthcare Review Butler Hospital Undertakes First Funded Study On The Impact of Exercise In Addiction Recovery Oct. 2004 <http://www.healthcarereview.com/back_issues/articles.php?show=190>*

my living room. The dog thought I was nuts, but I had a ball.

You can do the same. Introduce some variety into your exercise program, but however you do it, plan on fitting in a simple workout three times a week into your life, especially when you get started. If you are completely sedentary, you'll want to begin slowly, and of course, be sure to discuss your exercise program with your doctor before you start, as he or she can provide specific guidelines tailored to your health condition, weight, lifestyle, and other important factors.

Remember also, the words of Dr. Robert N. Butler of Mount Sinai Medical School in New York: "If exercise could be packaged into a pill, it would be the single most prescribed and beneficial medicine in the nation."

Part Five: Diet

If I were brutally honest and had to write my own diet plan for this book it would be embarrassingly simple: eat healthy, avoid sugar, and drink boatloads of water. It worked for me: I achieved my goal of moderation, dropped an awful lot of weight, and dramatically improved my health.

However, people much smarter than me have more to say on the matter and suggest eliminating certain foods— while adopting others—to significantly help reduce cravings and put you on a solid path to recovery. For that reason, I'll tow the line and provide some of that information here.

According to the experts, during the recovery phase eating sugar in any form can be risky, including that found in fruit juices, as it simply promotes your craving to drink. I think it's true; in fact, I noticed when I first started the program and was no longer drinking several Screwdrivers each night, I had terrible sugar craving and desired carbohydrates like crazy. I could only imagine my body was adjusting to the sugars it was no longer getting in those evening cocktails. I didn't crave the drinks, but seemed hungry for pasta and bread.

However, once the program was underway, the nutritional supplements helped keep my system in check, and I transitioned by allowing myself to eat more bagels and other breads, at least early on.

Speaking of which, refined carbohydrates are another no-no. White bread and rice, mashed potatoes, canned vegetables, pastries, and other items in this category have limited nutritional value, and even worse, assault your body with a mega dose of glucose, which results in—you guessed it—sugar cravings.

You should opt instead for high-fiber whole foods such as fresh vegetables, brown rice, fruits, nuts, honey, soybeans, and fish, all of which provide desirable nutrients, helping to keep blood sugar stable and cravings at bay.

You should eat regular healthy meals and small snacks, which will also help keep glucose levels stable during the day. Again, drink copious amounts of water, and limit your intake of coffee or other caffeinated beverages. (I never start the day without one or two cups of coffee, but decided to forgo my teaspoon of sugar in each. I hardly missed it once I started the program). You probably will not want carbonated drinks once you start taking topiramate, at first anyway, because that funny taste on your tongue is one of the medication's quirky side effects.

And cut back on deserts so you don't find yourself craving more sugars, which could lead to excessive drinking in the evening. Much of this will probably come naturally once you start the program, as your cravings for sweets in general will be reduced.

Of course, consult your physician before making modifications to your diet or undertaking any other part of this program.

CHAPTER **FIVE**

> *To tend unfailingly, unflinchingly,*
> *towards a goal, is the secret of success.*
> *–Anna Pavlova*

GETTING STARTED

*P*repare to change your life. Believe it or not, the operative word here is "prepare" because it will make for a much more organized and effective program if you have everything planned, purchased, and ready to go.

And remember, this is an integrative system—all elements work synergistically to get you through the withdrawal, past your cravings, and on to a new and healthy lifestyle. It's also extremely important that you are ready in both body and spirit to make this transformation. Motivation is absolutely critical.

READY...

1) Schedule an appointment with your physician

During your visit, explain that you are about to begin a program to improve your health by cutting back or completely eliminating alcohol from your life. In addition to a check-up, explain why you believe this program would be helpful to you, as it has been to others. Discuss topiramate (which is covered by most insurance plans) and see whether or not your doctor feels it is right for you. You may wish to bring a copy of *The Lancet* article, or other materials referred to earlier, in the event your physician is unfamiliar with topiramate's use as an anti-craving medication.

And note: if you feel your doctor would dismiss an integrative approach such as this, or would dissuade you from pursuing a therapy incorporating hypnosis or other elements of this program, it may be time to find another provider. There has never been a more critical time for you to take an aggressive and proactive approach to your health care.

2) Order the hypnotherapy CDs

The four-set CD series customized for this program costs $98, which is an excellent value. (My set was originally $298 since I wrote the script from scratch.) You may purchase them securely from the hypnotherapist at www.hypnotictapes.com. I am not involved in the transaction, nor do I receive a commission on sales. Look for the "My Way Out" title under Control/Stop Alcohol Use.

If you are absolutely unable to afford the the four CDs, which include the titles "Clearing", "Hypnotic", "Subliminal" and "Sleep Learning", consider purchasing

"Hypnotic" alone for $28 to gain what the hypnotherapist terms "major benefit." This book assumes you will use all four for "maximum benefit", but you can modify the program with the single recording.

3) Purchase the vitamins, minerals, and supplements

Most products should be relatively easy to find as long as you have a major grocery chain, drug store, and/or health food store in your community. If you are unable to find any of the nutritional items, please visit my website at www.mywayout.org for links to online resources. Try to not substitute inferior products for those that are recommended.

While you're awaiting the arrival of your CDs and doctor's appointment, there are a number of other details to tend to. Pull out a calendar and think about your schedule for the next several weeks. I find it's best to start this program in an absolutely focused state of mind and at a time when you can be extremely committed to the program. Make sure you'll not be interrupted with business travel, houseguests, excessive office hours, or any planned major events, at least for the first couple of weeks.

Also, if you have a family, think about who you can tell what in your household before you begin, because it is infinitely easier to do—though not impossible—if someone is there to support you.

It can be taxing to make excuses about the new vitamins you're consuming (children become easily alarmed if they believe you are taking new medicines because you're sick) and it's difficult to sneak behind closed doors to listen to the hypnotic CDs, as they require you to put your life on hold, if only for half hour sessions.

The latter may seem like a minor detail, but truly, it is easier if a partner or older child knows you are not to be disturbed so you can fully relax, and not worry that someone will bust into your bedroom or study and interrupt your hypnotherapy sessions.

Again, these incidental challenges are usually satisfied with easy workarounds, but it's helpful to prepare so you can quell worrisome family members or carve out private time where you can count on being alone, quiet, and relaxed. The rewards are infinite when your clan gets "the real you" back.

Other important items to purchase if you don't already have them on hand include:

- A CD player for listening to the hypnotic recordings (they are also available in audio cassette).
- A quality pair of headphones (I prefer the noise cancellation type) that can be worn comfortably when reclining. Make sure they cover your ears.
- A large capacity pill box—one that has four vertical and seven horizontal rows
- A smaller and discreet pill box for taking in your purse, briefcase or bag during the day
- A water bottle to have with you at all times whether at home or the office. (Buy a new one in a fun

color or with a special logo that is yours alone and reminds you of this wonderful and positive change you're making!)

- A CD player at your bed stand or in your bedroom that has an "endless loop" feature so you can run the Sleep Learning CD all night.
- A CD player in your car, home or office so you can play the Subliminal CD each day. This is very important because it contains the post-hypnotic cues you'll be given during the first 30 days of the program while your brain is being retrained. Incidentally, the CD will play in most computers with a sound card, so it can be run in the background while you work at your desk.

SET...

When I first considered the daunting number of supplements I needed to incorporate into an effective program—and frankly, which added up to approximately the same amount as those in the plans I had rejected earlier—I was stumped. Yet I knew a legitimate therapy wouldn't be complete without them.

I had also faced the problem of simply trying to *find* some of the products I needed in my local stores.

But a well-informed nutritionist provided me with an elegant solution and one which I'd not considered earlier—though admittedly it had not been available to such a wide degree before. She suggested I consider using a high quality nutritional powder that included most of the potent and desirable ingredients I was looking for. What it lacked for my specific purposes, I could easily add in pill or tablet form, which is exactly what I did.

I evaluated a number of powder (not strict protein) supplement products on the market and settled on Nutritech's ALL ONE®. I found it attractive because of its quality, price and availability. The formula can be found in many supermarket chains or on the web. The Original Formula is least expensive and great for women who are still menstruating, but contains 18 mg. of iron, which may be considered excessive for men or menopausal women. I recommend they purchase the Fruit Antioxidant or Active Seniors Formula. There are other blends, as well, and the company offers a discount to our readers on the entire line of products. You can learn more about it on page 153 in the Appendix.

You should be able to purchase everything else on my list of 'supplementary' supplements in most drug, grocery, or health food stores. I've included the brand name of the products I used or recommended so you know exactly what to look for or can ask for comparable quality brands.

The advantage of this system is that it does not require you to take handfuls of supplements every few hours—something I simply couldn't tolerate. You will drink the ALL ONE® Powder in the morning when you take your topiramate, and for the next month and a half, will swallow only six supplements through the day, divided into four doses: mid-morning, lunch, dinner and bedtime.

When you up your dose of topiramate, you'll take it during the day, as well. (I've provided a chart later in this chapter to make it easy to track). If topiramate makes you sleepy, you should take the second dose late at night. At the end of the six-week period, you are no longer required to take the additional supplements. You simply drink ALL ONE® in the morning, and take topiramate later. That's all there is to it.

A list of all the supplements you need follows. It's not imperative you use the same company's products, as long as you match the exact dosages and don't substitute the nutritional powder. I have not contacted any of the manufacturers below about this program, but recognize them to be providers of high quality products. (Don't skimp!) Here's what you'll need:

1) Nutritech ALL ONE® Powder: Original, Fruit Antioxidant or Active Seniors Formula
2) Nature's Way® B-50 Complex with B2 Co-enzyme
3) Naturally Preferred ™ Magnesium, 250 mg.
4) Solaray® Kudzu Root Extract, 150 mg.
5) Nature's Way® Milk Thistle Extract 175 mg./ Blessed Thistle, 180 mg. (You may substitute with Milk Thistle alone)
6) Royal Brittany™ Evening Primrose Oil, 1300 mg.
7) Hyland's™ Calms Forte Sleep Aid

If you're unable to find any of the supplements mentioned above in your local stores, you shouldn't have any problem doing so online. Kudzu extract, for example, may be difficult to locate in capsule format and while less convenient to dispense in its fine powder, it is critical to the program. If your health food store carries the powder and nothing else, and you don't want to purchase capsules online, go ahead and buy it locally, find out how to measure equivalent amounts, and simply mix it into your soup, salsa, and other foods. It has little flavor.

When you have all the supplements together, it's important to organize them for the week and then plan on doing this every seven days—say, on Sunday night if you work a regular Monday through Friday job. There's nothing worse than clamoring through you medicine chest looking for this supplement or that vitamin—or learning at an inconvenient moment that you've run completely out. (Keep in mind that you'll need to replenish your supply of some supplements before your six-week period is up.)

Using the chart on the page 118—which you may wish to photocopy and keep in your vitamin cupboard—fill your vitamin container with your supplements and topiramate for the first of your six weeks, and, again, plan to repeat the process weekly. Depending on your work schedule, transfer those you'll need during the part of the day or week you'll be out of the house to your smaller, portable pill container. (Or fill both large and small containers beforehand to accommodate your schedule if it's more convenient.)

If you're home all day, or are comfortable taking the large pill caddy to your office—and will have it with you all day—it won't be necessary to make the transfer from large to small container.

The day of reckoning usually arrives when that final piece is put into place: the CD's arrive in the mail; the final supplements are purchased; or the doctor's visit is over and the prescription is filled. I find that once patients have their topiramate in hand, they are much relieved. It seems to be a major psychological hurdle, although the prescribing of off-label pharmaceuticals is a much more common practice than many people realize and physicians, many of whom now know about topiramate's efficacy in treating problem drinking, are generally enthusiastic about the program.

The topiramate protocol you'll be following is, after all, based on a successful, double blind study published in a highly esteemed, peer-reviewed medical journal led by a world-class research team.

And that's nothing to snort at.

Nutritional Supplements Dosing & Schedule

	Breakfast/ After	Mid-Morning	Lunch/ After	Dinner/ After	Bedtime
All One Powder®	Heaping Tablespoon				
B-50 Formula		1 capsule			
Kudzu*		1 x 150 mg	1 x 150 mg	1 x 150 mg	
Milk Thistle/ Blessed Thistle*		175 mg/ 180 mg	175 mg/ 180 mg	175 mg/ 180 mg	
Magnesium			250 mg	250 mg	
Evening Primrose Oil		1,300 mg	1,300 mg		
Calms Forte**		Take 2	Take 2	Take 1	Take 1
Topamax®	See chart				

* Best taken between meals

** Consult with your doctor about modifying the amount of Calms Forte you take if it makes you sleepy. (Topiramate also makes some people feel fatigued, at least when dosing up.) However, It can be helpful in reducing the anxiety some experience during the early withdrawal phase, or assist with sleep during the first week or so, if necessary. Some individuals stop using it completely at the third or forth week.

Notes and observations:

_____

_____

_____

_____

_____

_____

_____

Topiramate Dose Escalation Schedule and Weight Loss Chart

Week	Morning dose	Afternoon dose	Total daily dose	Weight
1	0 mg	1x25 mg tablet	25 mg	
2	0 mg	2x25 mg tablets	50 mg	
3	1x25 mg tablet	2x25 mg tablets	75 mg	
4	2x25 mg tablets	2x25 mg tablets	100 mg	
5	2x25 mg tablets	1x100 mg tablet	150 mg	
6	1x100 mg tablet	1x100 mg tablet	200 mg	
7	1x100 mg tablet	1x100 mg and 2x25 mg tablets	250 mg	
8	1x100 mg and 2x25 mg tablets	1x100 mg and 2x25 mg tablets	300 mg	
9	1x100 mg and 2x25 mg tablets	1x100 mg and 2x25 mg tablets	300 mg	
10	1x100 mg and 2x25 mg tablets	1x100 mg and 2x25 mg tablets	300 mg	
11	1x100 mg and 2x25 mg tablets	1x100 mg and 2x25 mg tablets	300 mg	
12	1x100 mg and 2x25 mg tablets	1x100 mg and 2x25 mg tablets	300 mg	

The topiramate dosing schedule above is the one used by START Center researchers in their clinical trial, which they based on the Physicians' Desk Reference 2000 Edition. I've added a "Weight" column, as I found it helpful (and rewarding) to track my weight loss during this period and after.

If you find topiramate's side effects bothersome and are not able to adequately address them with the supplements on page 131, you may wish to dose up more slowly by starting with Topiramate Sprinkles®, available in 15 mg. capsules. As always, discuss dose escalation, or any other aspects of the program, with your physician.

Notes and observations:

_____

_____

_____

GO...!

The time is finally here. You're ready to jump in and make the change. Maybe like me, you also know deep down inside, even before you begin, that it's going to work. You've already done the hardest part by committing to lower or eliminate your alcohol intake. Now you're ready to begin the exciting stuff!

Remember your commitment to yourself on days when you don't feel like exercising, "can't make time" for hypnotherapy, or feel "it's okay" to skip your supplements or medication. Because no matter how passionately you want it, it's still going to be work—or at the very least, a hassle—on some days. But if you're looking for positive, sustainable success, you'll need to stick with this program and make it a priority.

The hypnotherapy, in particular, must be done for several consecutive weeks to reinforce the new patterns and habits you may enjoy fairly early in the program while topiramate is busy ramping up to "rewire" your brain. The Texas researchers found significant differences between self-reported and objective drinking indicators in the topiramate and placebo group at six and eight weeks, but you'll have an added benefit of hypnotherapy, nutritional supplements, and exercise, so it's unlikely you'll have to wait so long.

The point is this: keep at it and remember the first phase is somewhat intensive but certainly doable: six weeks of downing a lot of vitamins, a month of listening to a lot of hypnotherapy and three days a week of taking a lot of brisk walks—or whatever it is you like to do for activity.

You should feel so incredibly different after only two weeks, you probably won't know what hit you. By two months, you'll be a whole new person. And two years? Maybe you'll be the one with a book to share.

What follows is a proposed weekly plan, which can be used as a guideline, but easily modified depending on your circumstances. For instance, you can listen to the hypnotherapy mid-day instead of evening, if you prefer (bedtime worked best for me, as I would turn off the CD player before coming out of hypnosis and simply drift into the most restful sleep I'd had in years) or drink the nutritional powder at a time other than breakfast.

It is also assumed you will take topiramate according to the chart on page 119. If you follow the recommended schedule, you will take one dose at weeks one and two, and will begin taking twice daily doses at the third week.

And a note to those of you who select moderation as a plan: consider starting out with a one, two, or up to four-week abstinence period and setting a weekly drinking limit afterwards. The Moderation Management program supports a 30-day abstinence approach and provides helpful information at their website.

Now on to the program, which is divided into three basic phases, which are presented on the following pages.

WEEKS ONE THROUGH FOUR

Supplements and Topiramate:

Breakfast: ALL ONE® Powder and appropriate dose of topiramate at week three and four (weeks one and two are afternoon doses only)

Mid-morning: B50, Kudzu, Milk Thistle, Evening Primrose Oil, Calms Forte

Lunch: Kudzu, Milk Thistle, Magnesium, Evening Primrose Oil, Calms Forte

Dinner: Kudzu, Milk Thistle, Magnesium, Calms Forte

Bedtime: Calms Forte

Exercise:

15-20 minutes of aerobic exercise such as brisk walking, swimming or other activity at least once three days a week. Consider using a CD player with upbeat music if appropriate to the activity.

Hypnotherapy Recordings:

Day 1: Listen to Clearing Tracks One★ (30 minutes) and Two★ (30 minutes); Sleep to Sleep Learning★★ (60 minutes)

Day 2: Listen to Subliminal★★★ (60 minutes); Listen to Hypnotic Tracks One★ (45 minutes) and Two★ (20 minutes); Sleep to Sleep Learning

★ With headphones   ★★ Without headphones on endless loop
★★★ Without headphones in background

Day 3: Listen to Subliminal and Sleep to Sleep Learning.

Day 4: Listen to Subliminal; Listen to Clearing Track Two; Sleep to Sleep Learning

Day 5: Listen to Subliminal; Sleep to Sleep Learning

Day 6: Listen to Subliminal: Listen to Hypnotic Track Two; Sleep to Sleep Learning

Day 7: Listen to Subliminal: Sleep to Sleep Learning
Repeat each week

This is a recommended schedule, but do what you feel works best, accommodates your schedule, and is what you will stick with.

Creating a Successful Hypnotherapy Program

According to the hypnotherapist, the recordings must be listened to for a minimum of 21-30 consecutive days for a behavior to become a habit. Track One of Clearing prepares your subconscious for Track Two, which reduces negative energy and resistance to the suggestions.

You can create a more powerful experience by considering beforehand—visualizing and perceiving in your mind's eye—what it is you wish to accomplish before you even begin. Tracks One and Two, as well as the others, will require your absolute and undivided attention, so make sure you can do them when you will not be disturbed and can place yourself in a very relaxed position. A dimly lit or darkened room is recommended.

You'll follow the Clearing sessions with Hypnotic, Subliminal, and Sleep Learning recordings. The Hypnotic tracks will guide you deep into hypnosis and will place the suggestions into your subconscious. Some individuals play one or both Hypnotic tracks during the day—and later find themselves very refreshed, as if they've taken a lengthy nap. Others use them just before bedtime. If you wish to listen before retiring, simply stop the CD before "counting back" just as the hypnotist instructs, and you will nod off to a very restful slumber. (Despite what some people think, you're still "conscious" while under hypnosis and able to perform such acts if you wish.)

The Subliminal recording should be played daily and at whatever volume you prefer. You do not have to pay any particular attention to it. It contains post-hypnotic cues which you cannot consciously hear, but are very effective.

Sleep Learning is played at low volume in continuous mode during your entire sleep cycle so that the suggestions are implanted deep into your subconscious.

One of the many benefits of the hypnotherapy program is a striking change in sleep patterns for many insomniacs. Some individuals find they are finally able to enter and remain in a deep and restful sleep for the first time in years.

Hypnotic Cues

As you've read, you'll be asked to furnish positive

suggestions and visualizations during your hypnotic sessions, so it's extremely helpful to prepare for this. Think beforehand about what "the new you" is up to. Visualize it—visualize you. See yourself clearly, meditate on it, and then share it with your subconscious during your highly suggestive hypnotic state (don't worry, you'll know exactly when you're there). The post-hypnotic cues will activate behavioral changes when you're not even looking.

You'll have an entire month of opportunities to plant positive images and visualizations during your hypnotherapy sessions, many of which will be highly personalized to your circumstances. For instance, some of you are planning a program of moderation, and others, abstinence.

Either way, there may be times when you'll find it helpful to draw upon or modify some of the suggestions from the list below. Be sure to use the journal pages in the back of the book to jot down your own ideas when you think of them.

Sample Visualizations:

For A Plan of Moderation:

I am fit and strong because I do not drink to excess.
I often do not want a second drink.
I sip slowly when I drink.
My home life is happier now that I drink moderately.

For a Plan of Abstinence:

I do not want to put liquor in my body.
I prefer to _____ rather than to drink alcohol.

My home life is happier now that I don't drink.

My craving to drink alcohol is simply gone.

For Either Plan:

I often crave water—it is the most refreshing and desirable drink for me.

I forget to want to drink alcohol.

I am the most sober person at any gathering and that's exactly how I want to be.

Sample Visualizations:

I see myself with a new energy level, getting all kinds of new tasks accomplished.

I see myself telling the waiter I don't want a drink, and meaning it.

I see myself looking forward to going for my walk, and feeling energized by it.

I see myself ordering sparkling water or another non-alcoholic drink, and thoroughly enjoying it.

The sound of _____ now reminds me of/that _____.

The sight of _____ now reminds me of/that _____.

The thought of _____ now reminds me of/that _____.

Again, these are merely starting points for your own suggestions and visualizations. Be creative and look always for new opportunities to create positive and effective strategies during your hypnotherapy sessions.

WEEKS FOUR THROUGH SIX

Supplements, Topiramate and Exercise

Continue to take the supplements and medication according to the charts on pages 118 and 119. Make time for invigorating exercise three times per week.

Hypnotherapy Recordings

Transition into fewer sessions or discontinue, if desired. At this point, you'll be quite familiar with each CD and will have a good sense of your progress, so will be comfortable making this decision.

WEEKS SIX THROUGH TWELVE

Supplements, Topiramate and Exercise

You may discontinue taking the supplements except for ALL ONE® Powder, unless your cravings remain strong. You should incorporate the vitamin powder, or an equivalent, into a lifelong nutritional regimen. Continue taking topiramate according to the dosing schedule, and exercise regularly.

Hypnotherapy Recordings

Optional only; listen if you wish to reinforce earlier sessions.

WEEKS TWELVE AND AFTER

Supplements, Topiramate and Exercise

Continue to take ALL ONE® Powder. Consult with doctor regarding dosing down topiramate; discontinuing, or simply remaining at current dosage, as many patients do. If you stop taking the medication, your physician will probably recommend you reduce your dosage by 25-50 mg. every four our five days or possibly more slowly. Continue to exercise.

Hypnotherapy Recordings

Again, optional, but consider using occasionally. An excellent long-term maintenance plan is to listen to the 16-minute Clearing recording once a month.

Helpful Suggestions to Keep You On Track:

ALL ONE® Powder

Some people love the powder; for others it's an acquired taste. The manufacturer recommends drinking it with juice, and many people mix it with orange juice, but I was reluctant to do so because it reminded me of the cocktail that got me into trouble every night all those years and the juice was loaded with fructose. But others insist on having it with OJ, and it works just fine for them. Your call.

One woman I know simply stirs hers with water every morning, but I could never tolerate drinking it in such a raw form, which turns brown if left unattended for very long. I eventually began to mix mine with "Spicy Hot" V8® Vegetable Juice, and quickly got hooked. I don't find it too spicy, but do find it loaded with Beta Carotene, Vitamin A, Vitamin C, and lycopene, which is what gives tomatoes their red color and has been associated with a reduced risk in certain kinds of cancer. My husband and I throw our ALL ONE® into the blender with V8® and knock it back every single morning.

ALL ONE®'s website lists a number of smoothie recipes for those who prefer a more rich and creamy start to their day. Be sure to experiment until you find something you know will work for you and that you'll stick with. The formula is absolutely loaded with a broad spectrum of vitamins and essential trace elements, as well as that critical profile of amino acids to help reduce craving.

Hypnotherapy

At the end of the 30 days, you may wish to take a break from the regular hypnotherapy sessions, but keep in mind it's a powerful tool available to you if you ever feel your craving sneaking back. Be vigilant! Listen to your own inner voice, and be flexible; if you feel you're getting bogged down in your routine, pull out the CDs and listen to them again; you may be surprised at how comforting and familiar they are after shelving them for a while.

Consider having a new subliminal CD produced with

different music for a change of pace, or sit down and brainstorm on new, positive suggestions and visualizations to reinforce the progress you've made.

Water

Water, water, everywhere—that should be your mantra! It will help flush out toxins, prevent kidney stones, promote weight loss, support your exercise program, improve your energy level, and minimize side effects. What is not to love about this cheap and readily available resource?

Side Effects

Unlike many who are prescribed topiramate for other ailments and who may suffer a number of side effects, you'll benefit from a potent integrative nutritional program that should prevent such symptoms. However, as I've noted earlier, don't be surprised if you experience a few of them, and the chart on the next page can help, although you may need to do some tweaking until you find what works best. The side effects that follow are representative of those reported by patients prescribed topiramate for off-label use in treating a number of afflictions, including bipolar disorder and binge eating. Don't be afraid to make changes to the regimen, but as always, just be sure to get your physician's approval before modifying your treatment plan.

Reported Side Effects (Anecdotal) and How to Alleviate Them

Symptom	Treatment
Tingling of the extremities	• Two 50 mg tablets Grape Seed Extract daily • Eat one to two bananas each day which will increase your potassium intake; they each contain approximately 400 mg
Hair loss, thinning or texture change	• One 200 mcg Selenium tablet daily • Two 1000 mcg Biotin tablets daily • Rogaine™, .05% massaged directly into the scalp • One to two 10 mcg organic zinc lozenges daily • Regular consumption of green tea
Anxiety	• Increase dosage of Calms Forte • Reduce intake of caffeinated beverages
Lethargy	• 100 mg Co-enzyme 10Q
Insomnia	• One mg tablet Melatonin before bedtime • Take Topiramate earlier in day if it causes sleeplessness
Cognitive Deficits	• Reduce dosing schedule of Topiramate if cognitive symptoms are severe and accompanied by other intolerable side effects • With physician's approval, consider short-term use of a nootropic such as Adrafinil (available online) or Modafinil, sold in U.S. drug and health food stores

Notes and observations:

_____

_____

_____

_____

_____

_____

MY WAY OUT

CHAPTER **SIX**

The best and safest thing is to keep a balance in your life, acknowledge the great powers around us and in us. If you can do that, and live that way, you are really a wise man.

–Euripides

LONG TERM MAINTENANCE

*T*he brain is incredible, capable of continually developing new neurological pathways. But don't let this clever organ inadvertently sabotage your efforts. Remember: you are wired fundamentally differently from those who never suffer the intense alcohol cravings that you have, and the transformation that has taken place in your life is relatively new.

That's why you must be vigilant in monitoring changes—even subtle ones—in your drinking behavior. (They won't be so subtle if you've opted for abstinence and have begun to drink again.) Listen to that little voice in your head, and be brutally honest if you start reverting to past behaviors.

If you observe anything that seems to indicate you are, in fact, slipping, you should do an honest assessment. If you've chosen moderation, you probably need to evaluate whether or not you're heading towards a serious setback and think long and hard about whether total abstinence is a more appropriate choice.

The most effective way to ensure you don't undo all the progress you've made in the last several weeks—and assuming you've continued drinking the nutritional powder—is to consider augmenting your plan with some of the other supplements, the medication, or other elements from the original program phase. If you discontinued taking topiramate and noticed a profound difference after doing so, talk to your medical provider about renewing your prescription. The same goes for the nutritional products. For example, add kudzu extract and/or Evening Primrose Oil to your daily plan.

I believe it is essential to continue drinking the ALL ONE® and can only assume that in addition to the other benefits, the amino acids provide a powerful means of keeping cravings in check. Individuals who "canned the can" told me afterwards they were surprised at how much easier it was to support their long term maintenance program once they returned to drinking the powdered supplement each day. If cost is an issue, don't forget the discount information on page 153; it can certainly make a difference over the long term, and the company charges very little for shipping.

Be sure to revisit the hypnotherapy program if you've discontinued it. Others have reported to me that a simple "20-minute tune-up" with the second track of the Hypnotic recording, done once each month and used in conjunction with the medication and/or nutritional powder, and exercise, is all they need to keep the craving at bay.

Consider new therapies, both traditional and alternative. Replace coffee with green tea, which provides anti-oxidants, and just as importantly, can be a powerful weapon in reducing your desire for sweets or alcohol. Look into auriculotherapy, which has its roots in ancient Chinese acupuncture. This highly effective non-invasive procedure stimulates specific points in the ear and is used to relieve pain and treat addictive behaviors.

And don't forget the importance of a recovery support program—one that fits your lifestyle and comfort level. You may wish to join a local fellowship-based gathering, or prefer to chat, or even "lurk" anonymously, online. You are always welcome to do so at the discussion board at www.mywayout.org.

Again, keep the hypnotherapy program close at hand. You need not listen to the recordings as intensively as you did earlier. In fact, at this point, you may want to have your own custom script embedded within the hypnosis sessions, with long-term maintenance goals you can write yourself. Try the monthly "20-minute tune up" or consider ordering subliminal CDs with music from your collection to play while you work or relax. (My personal favorite is one I made from my Andrea Bocelli CDs. I never tire of listening to it.) The subliminal recordings will continue to provide the powerful post-hypnotic cues that help keep your brain re-wired. Also play the Sleep Learning CDs at night occasionally.

As simple as it may sound, eat well, get adequate rest and keep stress under control. This will go a long way in helping to avoid a potential relapse. And don't forget the importance of making time for a little exercise in your weekly schedule.

How incredible we live in an age when integrative approaches to medicine are finally gaining the respect they deserve. And how disheartening to think about all of those who have gone before us who tried with all their might to control their drinking but failed because they didn't have the knowledge or proper tools to make it work.

You now have both.

Use them wisely, help build on the body of knowledge by documenting your experience, and never forget the commitment you made that allowed you to begin this journey.

Taken altogether, they will change your life.

APPENDIX A

MODERATE DRINKING

t has been said that nine out of ten problem drinkers actively avoid traditional approaches to treatment. And that they will make better informed choices about moderation or abstinence goals based on the experience of others, as well as information gained through education.

In this book I have shared my experience, that of others, and information about a program I am absolutely convinced works. I also feels it's important to include material from recognized, highly regarded sources, such as the National Institute on Alcohol Abuse and Alcoholism, with this overview about the pros and cons of moderate drinking. Hopefully, this will help you make the best informed decision about what's right for you. RJ

Moderate Drinking
Reprinted with permission of NIAAA

Moderate drinking is difficult to define because it means different things to different people. The term is often confused with "social drinking," which refers to drinking patterns that are accepted by the society in which they occur. However, social drinking is not necessarily free of problems. Moderate drinking may be defined as drinking that does not generally cause problems, either for the drinker or for society. Since there are clearly both benefits and risks associated with lower levels of drinking, this Alcohol Alert will explore potentially positive and adverse effects of "moderate" drinking.

It would be useful if the above definition of moderate drinking were bolstered by numerical estimates of "safe" drinking limits. However, the usefulness of quantitative definitions of moderate drinking is compromised by the likelihood that a given dose of alcohol may affect different people differently. Adding further complexity, the pattern of drinking is also an important determinant of alcohol-related consequences. Thus, while epidemiologic data are often collected in terms of the "average number of drinks per week," one drink taken each day may have different consequences than seven drinks taken on a Saturday night[1].

Despite the complexity, numerical definitions of moderate drinking do exist. For example, guidelines put forth jointly by the U.S. Department of Agriculture and the U.S. Department of Health and Human Services[2] define moderate drinking as no more than one drink a day for most women, and no more than two drinks a day for most men. A standard drink is generally considered to be 12 ounces of beer, 5 ounces of wine, or 1.5 ounces of 80-proof distilled spirits. Each of these drinks contains roughly the same amount of absolute alcohol—approximately 0.5 ounce or 12 grams[3].

These guidelines exclude the following persons, who should not consume alcoholic beverages: women who are pregnant or trying to conceive; people who plan to drive or engage in other activities that require attention or skill; people taking medication, including over-the-counter medications; recovering alcoholics; and persons under the age of 21[2]. Although not specifically addressed by the guidelines, alcohol use also is contraindicated for people with certain medical conditions such as peptic ulcer.

The existence of separate guidelines for men and women reflects research findings that women become more intoxicated than men at an equivalent dose of alcohol[4]. This results, in part, from the significant difference in activity of an enzyme in stomach tissue of males and females that breaks down alcohol before it reaches the bloodstream. The enzyme is four times more active in males than in females[5]. Moreover, women have proportionately more fat and less body water than men. Because alcohol is more soluble in water than in fat, a given dose becomes more highly concentrated in a female's body water than in a male's[6].

Since the proportion of body fat increases with age, Dufour and colleagues recommend a limit of one drink per day for the elderly (7).

Benefits of Moderate Drinking

Psychological benefits of moderate drinking. A review of the literature[8] suggests that lower levels of alcohol consumption can reduce stress; promote conviviality and pleasant and carefree feelings; and decrease tension, anxiety, and self-consciousness. In the elderly, moderate drinking has been reported to stimulate appetite, promote regular bowel function, and improve mood[7].

Cardiovascular benefits of moderate drinking. There is a considerable body of evidence that lower levels of drinking decrease the risk of death from coronary artery disease (CAD). This effect has been demonstrated in a broad range of older epidemiologic studies[9]. More recently, Boffetta and Garfinkel[10] found that white American men who reported in 1959 that they consumed an average of fewer than three drinks per day were less likely to die during the next 12 years than men who reported abstinence. This finding was due primarily to a reduction in CAD. In a similar study using a wide range of ethnic groups, De Labry and colleagues[11] found that rates of overall mortality were lowest for men who consumed fewer than three drinks per day over a 12-year period.

Similar results have been obtained with female subjects. Stampfer and colleagues [12] analyzed data on middle-aged women and determined that consumption of approximately one drink per day decreases the risks of coronary heart disease. Razay and colleagues[13], using a random population sample, found consumption of up to two drinks per day to be associated with lower levels of cardiovascular risk factors in women. In postmenopausal women, the apparent protective effect of alcohol may be explained in part by an alcohol-induced increase in estrogen levels [14].

Various researchers have suggested that moderate drinking is not protective against CAD, arguing that higher mortality among abstainers results from including among them people who have stopped drinking because of ill health. Higher mortality among these "sick quitters" would explain the comparative longevity of moderate drinkers [15,16,17]. However, studies investigating the "sick quitter" effect do not support that conclusion; including "sick quitters" in the abstinent category cannot completely explain the apparent protective effect of moderate drinking against CAD [10,18,19,20].

Risks of Moderate Drinking

There are risks that might offset the benefits of moderate drinking. Research shows that adverse consequences may occur at relatively low levels of consumption[1].

Stroke. A review of epidemiologic evidence concludes that moderate alcohol consumption increases the potential risk of strokes caused by bleeding, although it decreases the risk of strokes caused by blocked blood vessels[21].

Motor vehicle crashes

While there is some evidence to suggest that low blood alcohol concentrations (BACs) bear little relationship to road crashes, impairment of driving-related skills by alcohol has been found to begin at 0.05 percent BAC or lower, with rapidly progressing deterioration as the BAC rises[22]. A man weighing 140 pounds might attain a BAC of 0.05 percent after two drinks.

Interactions with medications

Alcohol may interact harmfully with more than 100 medications, including some sold over the counter[23]. The effects of alcohol are especially augmented by medications that depress the function of the central nervous system, such as sedatives, sleeping pills, anticonvulsants, antidepressants, anti-anxiety drugs, and certain painkillers. There is a consequent increased danger of driving an automobile after even moderate drinking if such medications are taken [24]. In advanced heart failure, alcohol may not only worsen the disease, but also interfere with the function of medications to treat the disease[25].

Cancer

Although most evidence suggests an increased risk for certain cancers only among the heaviest drinkers, moderate drinking may be weakly related to female breast cancer. In one study[26], breast cancer was approximately 50 percent more likely to develop in women who consumed three to nine drinks per week than in women who drank fewer than three drinks per week. Although evidence concerning large bowel cancer is conflicting, one study suggests the possibility of a weak relation to consumption of one or more drinks per day[27].

Birth defects

Several ongoing studies are exploring the fetal risks associated with low levels of alcohol consumption. In one study[28], children whose mothers reported consuming an average of two to three drinks per day during pregnancy were smaller in weight, length, and head circumference and had an increased number of minor physical anomalies when examined at intervals through the age of 3. In addition, mothers' self-reported consumption of as few as two drinks per day during pregnancy was found to be related to a decrease in IQ scores of 7-year-old children[29].

The question of whether moderate drinking is a risk factor for the fetus is not altogether settled, because mothers' self-reports of alcohol consumption may be underestimates [30]. However, animal research provides additional evidence for adverse fetal effects from low levels of drinking. Nervous system abnormalities occurred in monkeys whose mothers were exposed weekly to low doses of alcohol. An effect occurred at a maternal BAC as low as 0.024 percent [31]. A 120-pound woman might attain this BAC after one drink. Similarly, low prenatal alcohol doses produced biochemical and physiological changes in rat brains[32,33].

Shift to heavier drinking

Recovering alcoholics, as well as people whose families have alcohol problems, may not be able to maintain moderate drinking habits[2]. Once a person progresses from moderate to heavier drinking, the risks of social problems (for example, drinking and driving, violence, trauma) and medical problems (for example, liver disease, pancreatitis, brain damage, reproductive failure, cancer) increase greatly [34].

References

(1) WERCH, C.E.; Gorman, D.R.; & Marty, P.J. Relationship between alcohol consumption and alcohol problems in young adults. Journal of Drug Education 17(3):261-276, 1987. (2) U.S. Department of Agriculture/U.S. Department of Health and Human Services. Home and Garden Bulletin No. 232. Nutrition and Your Health: Dietary Guidelines for Americans. 3d ed. Washingt on, DC: Supt. of Docs., U.S. Govt. Print. Off., 1990. (3) WHELAN, E.M. To your health. Across the Board, Jan. 1988, pp. 49-53. (4) JONES, B.M., & Jones, M.K. Alcohol effects in women during the menstrual cycle. Annals of the New York Academy of Sciences 273:576-587, 1976. (5) FREZZA, M.; Di Padova, C.; Pozzato, G.; Terpin, M.; Baraona, E.; & Lieber, C.S. High blood alcohol levels in women: The role of decreased gastric alcohol dehydrogenase activity and first-pass metabolism. New England Journal of Medicine 322(2):95-99, 1990. (6) GOIST, K.C., & Sutker, P.B. Acute alcohol intoxication and body composition in women and men. Biochemistry & Behavior 22:811-814, 1985. (7) DUFOUR, M.C.; Archer, L.; & Gordis, E. Alcohol and the elderly. Clinics in Geriatric Medicine 8(1):127-141, 1992. (8) BAUM-BAICKER, C. The psychological benefits of moderate alcohol consumption: A review of the literature. Drug and Alcohol Dependence 15:305-322, 1985. (9) MOORE, R.D., & Pearson, T.A. Moderate alcohol consumption and coronary artery disease: A review. Medicine 65(4):242-267, 1986. (10) BOFFETTA, P., & Garfinkel, L. Alcohol drinking and mortality among men enrolled in an American Cancer Society prospective study. Epidemiology 1(5):342-348, 1990. (11) DE LABRY, L.O.; Glynn, R.J.; Levenson, M.R.; Hermos, J.A.; LoCastro, J.S.; & Vokonas, P.S. Alcohol consumption and mortality in an American male population: Recovering the U-shaped curve—findings from the normative aging study. Journal of Studies on Alcohol 53(1):25-32, 1992. (12) STAMPFER, M.J.; Colditz, G.A.; Willett, W.C.; Speizer, F.E.; & Hennekens, C.H. A prospective study of moderate alcohol consumption and the risk of coronary disease and stroke in women. New England Journal of Medicine 319(5):267-273, 1988. (13) RAZAY, G.; Heaton, K.W.; Bolton, C.H.; & Hughes, A.O. Alcohol consumption and its relation to cardiovascular risk factors in British women. British Medical Journal 304:80-83, 1992. (14) GAVALER, J.S., & Van

Thiel, D.H. The association between moderate alcoholic beverage consumption and serum estradiol and testosterone levels in normal postmenopausal women: Relationship to the literature. Alcoholism: Clinical and Experimental Research 16(1):87-92, 1992. (15) MARMOT, M., & Brunner, E. Alcohol and cardiovascular disease: The status of the U shaped curve. British Medical Journal 303:565-568, 1991. (16) SHAPER, A.G. Alcohol and mortality: A review of prospective studies. British Journal of Addiction 85:837-847, 1990. (17) SHAPER, A.G.; Wannamethee, G.; & Walker, M. Alcohol and mortality in British men: Explaining the U-shaped curve. Lancet 2(8623):1267-1273, 1988. (18) KLATSKY, A.L.; Armstrong, M.A.; & Friedman, G.D. Risk of cardiovascular mortality in alcohol drinkers, ex-drinkers and nondrinkers. American Journal of Cardiology 66:1237-1242, 1990. (19) JACKSON, R.; Scragg, R.; & Beaglehole, R. Alcohol consumption and risk of coronary heart disease. British Medical Journal 303:211-216, 1991. (20) RIMM, E.B.; Giovannucci, E.L.; Willett, W.C.; Colditz, G.A.; Ascherio, A.; Rosner, B.; & Stampfer, M.J. Prospective study of alcohol consumption and risk of coronary disease in men. Lancet 338(8765):464-468, 1991. (21) CAMARGO, C.A., Jr. Moderate alcohol consumption and stroke: The epidemiologic evidence. Stroke 20(12):1611-1626, 1989. (22) Council on Scientific Affairs. Alcohol and the driver. Journal of the American Medical Association 255(4):522-527, 1986. (23) SHINN, A.F., & Shrewsbury, R.P., eds. Evaluations of Drug Interactions. New York: Macmillan, 1988. (24) GILMAN, A.G.; Rall, T.W.; Nies, A.S.; & Taylor, P., eds. Goodman and Gilman's The Pharmacological Basis of Therapeutics. New York: Pergamon Press, 1990. (25) THOMAS, B.A., & Regan, T.J. Interactions between alcohol and cardiovascular medications. Alcohol Health & Research World 14(4):333-339, 1990. (26) WILLETT, W.C.; Stampfer, M.J.; Colditz, G.A.; Rosner, B.A.; Hennekens, C.H.; & Speizer, F.E. Moderate alcohol consumption and the risk of breast cancer. New England Journal of Medicine 316:1174-1180, 1987. (27) KLATSKY, A.L.; Armstrong, M.A.; Friedman, G.D.; & Hiatt, R.A. The relations of alcoholic beverage use to colon and rectal cancer. American Journal of Epidemiology 128(5):1007-1015, 1988. (28) DAY, N.L.; Robles, N.; Richardson, G.; Geva, D.; Taylor, P.; Scher, M.; Stoffer, D.; Cornelius, M.; & Goldschmidt, L. The effects of prenatal alcohol use on the growth of children at three years of age. Alcoholism: Clinical and Experimental Research 15(1):67-71, 1991. (29) STREISSGUTH, A.P.; Barr, H.M.; & Sampson, P.D. Moderate prenatal alcohol exposure: Effects on child IQ and learning problems at age 7 1/2 years. Alcoholism: Clinical and Experimental Research 14(5):662-669, 1990. (30) ERNHART, C.B.; Morrow-Tlucak, M.; Sokol, R.J.; & Martier, S. Underreporting of alcohol use in pregnancy. Alcoholism: Clinical and Experimental Research 12(4):506-511, 1988. (31) CLARREN S.K.; Astley, S.J.; Bowden, D.M.; Lai, H.; Milam, A.H.; Rudeen, P.K.; & Shoemaker, W.J. Neuroanatomic and neurochemical abnormalities in nonhuman primate infants exposed to weekly doses of ethanol during gestation. Alcoholism: Clinical and Experimental Research 14(5):674-683, 1990. (32) FARR, K.L.; Montano, C.Y.; Paxton, L.L.; & Savage, D.D. Prenatal ethanol exposure decreases hippocampal 3H-glutamate binding in 45-day-old rats. Alcohol 5(2):125-133, 1988. (33) SWARTZWELDER, H.S.; Farr, K.L.; Wilson, W.A.; & Savage, D.D. Prenatal exposure to ethanol decreases physiological plasticity in the hippocampus of the adult rat. Alcohol 5(2):121-124, 1988. (34) National Institute on Alcohol Abuse and Alcoholism. Seventh Special Report to the U.S. Congress on Alcohol and Health. DHHS Pub. No. (ADM)90-1656. Washington, DC: Supt. of Docs., U.S. Govt. Print. Off., 1990.

APPENDIX B

ALCOHOLISM'S PROGRESSIVE STAGES

Alcoholism, the Illness and The Progressive Stages of Alcoholism
Cynthia Mascott, Licensed Mental Health Counselor
Reprinted with permission, PsychCentral.com, Copyright (c) 2001-2004

What is alcoholism? According to the American Medical Association, "alcoholism is an illness characterized by significant impairment that is directly associated with persistent and excessive use of alcohol. Impairment may involve physiological, psychological or social dysfunction." Psychologically speaking, alcoholism has less to do with "how much" someone is drinking, and more to do with what happens when they drink. If you have problems when you drink, you have a drinking problem.

The word alcohol comes from the Arabic "Al Kohl," which means "the essence." Alcohol has always been associated with rites of passages such as weddings and graduations, social occasions, sporting events and parties. The media has often glamorized drinking. Television viewers happily recount the Budweiser frog, the beach parties and general "good time" feeling of commercials selling beer. Magazine ads show beautiful couples sipping alcohol. Love, sex and romance are just around the corner as long as you drink the alcohol product being advertised.

The reality is that alcohol is often abused because it initially offers a very tantalizing promise. With mild intoxication, many people become more relaxed. They feel more carefree. Any preexisting problems tend to fade into the background. Alcohol can be used to enhance a good mood or change a bad mood. At first, alcohol allows the drinker to feel quite pleasant, with no emotional costs. As an individual's drinking progresses, however, it takes more and more alcohol to achieve the same high. Eventually the high is hardly present.

How Common is Alcoholism?

Alcoholism is a complex disease, which has been misunderstood and stigmatized. According to the American Psychiatric Association's Diagnostic and Statistical Manual of Mental Disorders, Fourth Edition (DSM-IV), Alcohol Dependence and Alcohol Abuse are among the most common mental disorders in the general population, with about eight percent of the adult population suffering from Alcohol Dependence and five percent from Alcohol Abuse.

It is widely accepted that there is a genetic predisposition toward alcoholism. According to DSM-IV, the risk for Alcohol Dependence is three to four times higher in close relatives of people with Alcohol Dependence.

The Progression of the Disease

Alcoholism is a progressive disease and follows several phases:

The Social Drinker

Social drinkers have few problems with alcohol. A social drinker can basically take or leave it. There is no preoccupation with drinking. A social drinker is able to control the amount of alcohol consumed and rarely drinks to the point of intoxication. For these individuals, drinking is a secondary activity. It is the party, the meal, the wedding that interests the social drinker, not the opportunity to drink.

The Early Stage

An individual who is experiencing the early stages of alcoholism will begin to have an assortment of problems associated with drinking. In the early stage alcoholism, a person may start to sneak drinks, begin to feel guilty about his or her drinking, and become preoccupied with alcohol. Blackouts, drinking to the point of drunkenness, and increased tolerance (needing more alcohol to achieve the same effect) are all signs of early alcoholism. An individual who is entering the early stage of alcoholism will seek out companions who are heavy drinkers and lose interest in activities not associated with drinking. Family and friends may begin to express concern about the person's consumption of alcohol. Work problems, such as missing work or tardiness, may also take place.

Middle Stage

By the time someone has entered the middle stages of alcoholism, his or her life has become quite unmanageable, although the alcoholic still denies that he/she has a problem. At this point, the alcoholic will often drink more than intended. He or she will drink in an attempt to erase feelings such as anger, depression and social discomfort. Drinking in the morning to relieve a bad hangover may also take place. The alcoholic's health care provider may begin to suggest that the alcoholic stop drinking. The individual may try to stop drinking, but without success. Job loss, medical problems, and serious family conflicts occur during this phase.

Late Stage

At this stage, the alcoholic's life has become completely unmanageable. Medical complications are numerous and include liver diseases such as cirrhosis or hepatitis. Acute pancreatitis (inflammation of the pancreas), high blood pressure, and a bleeding of the esophageal lining can result from prolonged use. The heart and brain are compromised so that an alcoholic is at a higher risking for either a heart attack or stroke. Depression and insomnia and even suicide are more prevalent at this stage. A condition known as Wernicke-Korsakoff Syndrome, which involves memory loss, indicates that the individual has sustained brain damage from drinking. A child born to a woman who drinks during her pregnancy may have a condition called fetal alcohol syndrome, causing a number of birth defects.

An alcoholic at this stage has become physically addicted to alcohol and will experience seizures or delirium tremens (DTs) if he or she stops drinking. It is extremely important to seek out medical care at this point in the disease process.

APPENDIX C

National Institute on Alcohol Abuse and Alcoholism
>   www.niaaa.nih.gov

My Way Out website
>   www.mywayout.org

Hypnotictapes.com
>   www.hypnotictapes.com

ALL ONE Supplement Powder
>   *www.all-one.com/mywayout.htm or call 800-235-5727*
>   *Note: My Way Out readers are provided a 15% product discount at the website above and the toll free number by using the code "MW15".*

The Lancet
>   www.thelancet.com
>   (search "oral topiramate alcohol dependence")

Addressing Alcoholism with Diet and Nutrition
>   www.holistichelp.net/alcoholism.html

Moderation Management
>   www.moderation.org

Notes & Journaling

Notes & Journaling

Notes & Journaling

Notes & Journaling

Notes & Journaling